AF522613

An Unlikely

POLICE CHIEF

From and To Jaisalmer House

An Unlikely

POLICE CHIEF

From and To Jaisalmer House

B.L. VOHRA IPS (RETD)

Konark Publishers Pvt Ltd

New Delhi

Konark Publishers Pvt Ltd
206, First Floor,
Peacock Lane, Shahpur Jat,
New Delhi - 110 049
+91-11-4105 5065
india@konarkpublishers.com, us@konarkpublishers.com
www.konarkpublishers.com

The photographs used in this book are from the author's collection.

ISBN: 978-81-956786-2-4

Edited by Dipali Singh
Cover jacket by Sanjeev Mathpal
Printed and bound at Thomson Press (India) Ltd

To

My grandchildren Shreya, Vansh, Tia, Ayaan, Aadit and Avi

Hope you experience and enjoy excellent health,
happiness, peace and prosperity in life…

Contents

Praise for the Book

This is the story of an honest refugee boy who overcomes the post-Partition challenges and succeeds in joining the IPS. Besides serving in Delhi and two Northeastern states, the author has the distinction of also serving in almost all the Central Armed Police Forces of the country! During the difficult times in his long career, this policeman refused to deviate from the straight and narrow, and yet rose to the highest position in the service. Those joining the constabularies will particularly benefit by reading this volume. Highly recommended!

N.N. VOHRA
Former Governor J&K

The autobiography of Shri B.L. Vohra, who is popular in the IPS fraternity as 'Bhushi' (an affectionate diminutive for Bhushan Lal Vohra), provides a rare instance of an IPS officer who has served in almost all Central police organizations and has done so with distinction. He proved his mettle during his stints as DGP of Manipur (where he was also the state Home Secretary), and Tripura, when the two Northeastern states were the theatre of insurgency and the state police forces were facing serious challenge in maintaining order and security. He led the police force in both states with distinction and the experience he gained there proved valuable during his term in the BSF, the CRPF, the CISF and in the elite NSG.

I had the good fortune to have Bhushi working with me in a district of the Delhi Police, where he began his career, and I could see that he was a sound professional. His varied experience of working with both the paramilitary forces and the state police forces have stood him in good stead.

Bhushi is blessed with a good pen which he has used well—rather prolifically—to author 13 books. His versatility was recognized when he was in the Delhi High Court's Monitoring Committee on Unauthorized Constructions and his public spiritedness is evident in the work of 'Vastradan', his NGO that collects clothes and distributes them among people who are below the poverty line, which by any means is a laudable effort.

His book is the story of his life that has been full of rich experiences and which should be both enjoyable reading and educative.

NIKHIL KUMAR

Former Governor of Nagaland and Kerala

Vohra's book about his journey from a little boy in a refugee camp on the outskirts of Delhi to the Director General of Police of two states, Manipur and Tripura, and also of two Central government organizations, Civil Defence and the Sashastra Seema Bal (SSB) makes easy reading.

Vohra has an easy style of writing after my own heart. He tells his story in a lucid language, which makes it an interesting reading. He is obviously prolific —he has 13 other books to his name!

What really struck me was that even if an assignment was a very uninteresting one with no chance of making any noticeable contribution, Vohra has not neglected to find avenues for amelioration. A good example of this is his contribution to rejuvenating the Civil Defence and Home Guards and putting new life into the Fire Brigade Services that prop up Civil Defence. His spirit of 'never say die' is also visible in the additional charge he held of the SSB just for a few months. In those few months he learnt that emoluments promised to the lowest ranks had not been paid! He cut through the red tape to the delight of the men!

This spirit of alleviating the sufferings of the lower ranks has been the hallmark of his leadership. It was bound to lift morale and boost group performance. So, when he retired and hung up his boots there were many who sought his services, including the Delhi High Court that appointed him on a panel to monitor demolition of unlicensed and illegally constructed structures on government and municipal lands.

Another feature that stands out in this story is his deep feelings of love and affection for his wife and his three daughters. The progress of the girls is minutely recorded at different stages of their journey through life. And unlike most of his contemporaries, the author and his wife seem to have found the time and the means to travel the world at regular intervals of time.

The real tough police work done by Vohra was in his parent cadre of Manipur-Tripura where he served off and on in short but memorable bursts. Before retiring, he headed the police forces of both these states in quick succession. By his accounts, he seemed to have done a commendable job of both assignments. His interactions with the politicians in both states will be of interest to young IPS officers entering service. It is always the most delicate part of our job but if one adheres to one's conscience and justice one should be able to come out unscathed. Vohra has spelt out in detail the operation he mounted against the underground elements in Tripura and neutralized the cadres operating in a certain specified area. That, too, should be of interest to police officers.

Many retired officers have begun writing their memoirs. It is a welcome development as their accounts of their own experiences represent living history. No experience, however small, is unimportant.

It will help young officers to learn and profit therefrom. And it is in that light that they should read this book.

JULIO F. RIBEIRO

Former Police Commissioner Mumbai

I have read with interest *An Unlikely Police Chief*, the autobiography of Shri B.L. Vohra, an illustrious police officer. An autobiography is a journey through time and so through a segment of history. In this case, it is through the tumults and tragedies of the Partition of India and picking up the threads of life and family in an Independent India. It is about building a career, dealing with abnormal situations on the eastern and the western flanks of our country and those in between. It is about navigating through the odds and evens of personal, professional and social life.

The book reflects the integrity and simplicity of the author with disarming humility, true to the elements that define the author. A police officer's life is replete with challenges, mostly unpredictable and often unseen. If not handled deftly, they can be ruinous to life and career of the officer. This book reveals a useful lesson that with politeness and humility one can be firm and unflinching on integrity in one's profession and still be successful.

This book distinguishes itself from other such works in ways it weaves the warps and woofs of the tapestry of life of a police officer without losing or underplaying the human being behind the uniform. It is a smooth and absorbing read. It will be especially useful to young and aspiring police officers.

—R.N. RAVI

Governor Tamil Nadu

Preface

I started writing this autobiography on 31 March 2020, the seventh day of the 21-day lockdown enforced by Prime Minister Narendra Modi in India due to the worldwide spread of the coronavirus. It also was the birthday of my eldest daughter, Archana.

Since we had to stay at home for most of the time to protect ourselves from the coronavirus, I utilized the lockdowns to write this book but with big gaps in between as at times I didn't feel like writing and was busy doing other activities. Finally, I completed it on the last day of 2021.

Questioning myself about why I was writing my autobiography, I struggled in my mind over a long period of time, considering the usefulness or otherwise of such an exercise. There are so many autobiographies in the world and I wondered who would be interested in mine. But the refrain from my close family and friends was that every individual's life story is unique; why should I not share mine? After all, in one life of 78 years, I had seen what seemed to span many centuries from what we can call a primitive life to a modern one with all its comforts in the 21st century. I am now living in an India totally different from an India in which I was born and grew up. Before Independence, Pakistan was part of India, but my family had to flee from there when the Partition of the subcontinent took place and live as refugees in India. My family and friends insisted that I should go ahead and share my experiences; so finally, I decided to take the plunge after 18 years of retirement because from a distance, one can look at life dispassionately.

I have been very lucky in life. With little effort I have come a long way. Since my life so far coincides with the life of India after Independence, I have seen its growth, ups and downs, and history in the making. Overall, India has done well and I'm proud of my country. I have also tried to touch on India's story in brief while penning my own memoir.

I hope readers will enjoy a peep into the past and present of not a distinguished but an ordinary person, his struggles, and his good luck due to the blessings of God and everybody else on this planet. It may inspire some.

New Delhi **B.L. Vohra, IPS (Retd)**

Acknowledgements

My memoir will be incomplete without conveying my gratitude to those who have helped me in the journey of my life. Starting with God, it is my parents, teachers, family, friends, colleagues and many more, including strangers, to whom I am thankful.

My special thanks to my wife Chander Jyoti, my daughters and their spouses—Archana and Rashi, Sonya and Rajnish, Manika and Anuj—and grandchildren Shreya, Vansh, Tia, Ayaan, Aadit and Avi, who have enriched my life, giving me immense support and joy, and now encouragement to write this autobiography. My wife had to maintain the utmost patience because of my mental absence while writing this book, even though I was at home.

My deepest gratitude to my cousin sister Bimla, my cousin brother K.K. Vohra, who passed away in January 2022, my wife's brother and sister, Satish and Neelam, and their families who have given me so much love and affection.

Among friends from my childhood, I will always be beholden to Ashok Chawla, his wife Kanwal, and Sudesh Kapoor, all of whom we lost to Covid-19, and Joginder Singh, who died a little earlier. My thanks to Karam Chand (aka Gulla), Pawan Kumar Gupta, Darshan Lal Sachdeva, Naginder Singh and S. Ramakrishnan and many more among my batchmates and other friends from the police service—and outside—with whom I am in touch. I am very grateful to Shri

N.N. Vohra, former Governor of Jammu and Kashmir, for the help and guidance he gave me many times.

I am grateful to many senior officers in my police profession who taught me a lot, even those who harassed me because I learnt something from them also. My gratitude goes to the various organizations I worked in or with over the years.

And thanks to my dear friend K.P.R. Nair, the publisher, for his encouragement and excellent work put in by him and his team for bringing out this book and my earlier publications.

Acronyms

ACP	Assured Career Progression
ACR	Annual Confidential Report
AD	Assistant Director
ADM	Additional District Magistrate
AFSPA	Armed Forces Special Powers Act
ASI	Assistant Sub-Inspector
ASP	Assistant Superintendent of Police
ATTF	All Tripura Tiger Force
BA	Bachelor of Arts
BJP	Bharatiya Janata Party
BOPs	Border Outposts
BPR&D	Bureau of Police Research and Development
BSF	Border Security Force
CAPFs	Central Armed Police Forces
CBI	Central Bureau of Investigation
CDI	Chief Drill Instructor
CEO	Chief Executive Officer
CGHS	Central Government Health Scheme
CID	Crime Investigation Department
CISF	Central Industrial Security Force
CO	Commandant/Commanding Officer
CoBRA	Commando Battalions for Resolute Action

CPEC	China–Pakistan Economic Corridor
CPM	Communist Party (Marxist)
CPTC	Central Police Training College
CPWD	Central Public Works Department
CRPF	Central Reserve Police Force
DC	Deputy Commissioner
DD	Deputy Director
DDA	Delhi Development Authority
DG or DGP	Director General of Police
DIG	Deputy Inspector General
DM	District Magistrate
DSP	Deputy Superintendent of Police
FIR	First Information Report
IAS	Indian Administrative Service
IB	Intelligence Bureau
ICRC	International Committee of the Red Cross
ICS	Indian Civil Service
IFS	Indian Foreign Service
IG	Inspector General
IIC	India International Centre
INA	Indian National Army
IPS	Indian Police Service
IRS	Indian Revenue Service
ISRO	Indian Space Research Organization
ITBP	Indo-Tibetan Border Police
ITI	Industrial Training Institute
J&K	Jammu and Kashmir
KCP	Kangleipak Communist Party
LDC	Lower Division Clerk
MA	Master of Arts
MCD	Municipal Corporation of Delhi

MGNREGA	Mahatma Gandhi National Rural Employment Guarantee Act
MLAs	Members of the Legislative Assembly
MMTC	Minerals and Metals Trading Corporation
MNPF	Manipur Naga People's Front
MP	Madhya Pradesh
NBCC	National Building Construction Corporation
NCC	National Cadet Corps
NDMA	National Disaster Management Authority
NDRF	National Disaster Management Force
NGO	Non-Governmental Organization
NIIT	National Institute of Information Technology
NLFT	National Liberation Front of Tripura
NSCN	National Socialist Council of Nagaland
NSG	National Security Guard
PAC	Provincial/Pradeshik Armed Constabulary
PLA	People's Liberation Army
PMO	Prime Minister's Office
POK	Pakistan-Occupied Kashmir
POP	Passing-Out Parade
PREPAK	People's Revolutionary Party of Kangleipak
PS	Principal/Private Secretary
PT	Physical Training
PTC	Police Training College
R&D	Research and Development
RAW	Research and Analysis Wing
RBI	Reserve Bank of India
RHE	Rajputana Hostel Estate
RSS	Rashtriya Swayamsevak Sangh
SC	Scheduled Caste
SDG	Special Duty Group

SDM	Sub-Divisional Magistrate
SDPOs	Sub-Divisional Police Officers
SHO	Station House Officer
SI	Sub-Inspector
SP	Superintendent of Police
SPOs	Special Police Officers
SSB	Sashastra Seema Bal
STC	State Trading Corporation
SVD	Samyukt Vidhayak Dal
TOM	Transit Officers' Mess
TSR	Tripura State Rifles
UDC	Upper Division Clerk
UN	United Nations
UNLF	United National Liberation Front
UP	Uttar Pradesh
UPA	United Progressive Alliance
UPSC	Union Service Public Commission
UT	Union Territory

Chapter 1

Childhood

On the evening of 30 September 1997, I was chatting with my counterpart Major General Saeed-ul-Hassan Zaidi of the Pakistan Rangers in the posh Lahore Mess of his paramilitary force that guarded the Pakistan border. 'Can a visit to Hasan Abdal be organized for me?' I asked him.

I was there as Inspector General (IG), BSF Jammu Frontier, as part of the Border Security Force (BSF) delegation for the six-monthly coordination meeting of the BSF with the Pakistan Rangers. He asked me, 'What is your special interest in the place?'

'I was born there, where the Panja Sahib gurudwara is located. You would know that this place, Hasan Abdal, is also known as Panja Sahib.'

Since many Indians who were born in Pakistan had moved over to India after the Partition, he was not surprised. He said, 'Sure. I'll work out the details.'

Of course, he never did so for some reason which I'll explain later in the book, but that longing to visit Panja Sahib still remains. So far, I haven't been able to go there.

I was born on 11 March 1944 in Panja Sahib[1] in Pakistan, located at about 65 kilometres north-west from Rawalpindi (also famously known as Pindi—the birthplace of the delicious Pindi *channa* or chickpeas), a city which is adjacent to Islamabad, the newly built capital of Pakistan. Located in a strategic part of northern Punjab, it was the point from where Mughal war expeditions were sent to the North-West Frontier. It was also visited by various Mughal emperors on their way to Kashmir. In modern times, this place, which lies at the intersection of the Karakoram Highway, serves as the terminus for the China–Pakistan Economic Corridor (CPEC) for its western alignment. It was always an important place.

The gurudwara there is known as Panja Sahib because of a handprint (*panja,* a Punjabi word, means the palm of a hand) engraved on a boulder at the gurudwara. It is believed to be that of Guru Nanak Dev Ji, the founder of Sikhism. Legend has it that in AD 1521, Guru Nanak and his disciple Bhai Mardana had halted in the present-day Hasan Abdal and began reciting *kirtan*s (devotional songs) under a tree that cast its shade over them, sheltering them from the scorching heat. People from in and around the village gathered around them, which annoyed a local saint, Shah Wali Qandhari. He refused to give water to Bhai Mardana to quench his thirst.

Observing this, the unperturbed Guru removed a big rock lying nearby. A fountain of pure freshwater sprang up from the soil and began to flow endlessly. Bhai Mardana, thus, quenched his thirst. At the same time, the saint's spring dried up. In a rage, he threw a boulder towards the Guru from the top of the hill. As it came hurtling down, the Guru stopped it with his hand, leaving a deep imprint on it. Observing the miracle, Wali became the Guru's devotee.

Later, Maharaja Ranjit Singh built a beautiful gurudwara near this

1. It is also known as Hasan Abdal, a place that houses one of the holiest shrines of the Sikhs.

boulder and pool as a token of gratitude and remembrance to the Guru. The gurudwara was named Panja Sahib by Hari Singh Nalwa, the famous Commander-in-Chief of the army of Ranjit Singh.

My family had settled there for many generations. I know this from the accounts of the family told to me by my father and from the ledgers kept by the family *pandit*s (priests) in pilgrim centres like Haridwar in Uttarakhand and Gaya in Bihar, which followed the tradition for over a century of writing the date of the visit of pilgrims along with the names of their family members.

When I visited Gaya in May 1979 for the *pind daan* (an offering to ancestors) of my father, I came across an entry in the ledger written in the Takra language about the visit of my great-grandfather Nanak Chand Vohra in 1919 and grandfather Dewan Chand Vohra in 1939 from Panja Sahib to Gaya for the *pind daan* of their forefathers. Looking at the present levels of comfort while travelling, it is difficult to imagine how their journey would have been over such a long distance in those times, especially in 1919.

Of course, I don't remember Panja Sahib because when the Partition of India took place in 1947, I was too young and my family had to leave that part of India which became Pakistan.

The Partition of India by the then British rulers was a big tragedy. Mainly, Punjab on the western and Bengal on the eastern side of India were divided, creating Pakistan in two parts, West and East Pakistan. During the Partition, millions got displaced when they had to move from one side to the other and this involved great suffering, including the violent loss of many lives and heinous crimes like brutal murders, rape, abduction, loot and forcible conversions. It was about 75 years ago now but the scars, though diminished significantly, still remain on the psyche. My father Shiv Ram Vohra, whom my three uncles and I used to call *Bhapaji* and mother Sheela Wanti Vohra, whom I used to call *Mata*, moved from that area towards India wearing only the barest of clothing. My mother told me that it was tremendously dangerous to be on the roads at the time since mobs had started killing Hindus and Sikhs in large numbers with gruesome violence. Looting, rapes and abduction were rampant in Panja Sahib and other areas that were to be included in Pakistan.

My family was hurriedly taken in a truck to the nearby Wah Army Cantonment, at a distance of about 9 kilometres from Panja Sahib where the army had established a refugee camp, which stretched its limits to accommodate about 12,000 persons in tents. They stayed there for quite some time. Then they went by a train to Amritsar. En route they saw many dead people killed with unimaginable brutality and rivers of blood all around. After reaching Amritsar with not even a paisa in their pockets, with me as a three-year-old toddler to look after, they lived in a refugee camp for about eight to ten days. They had to live in tents and make do with dry *chapati*s only once in roughly two days, which they would dip in water to make them soft enough to eat. They couldn't afford to buy anything because even one onion cost Rs 2 at that time! Those two rupees may be equivalent to more than Rs 200 of today.

When my family was told that they had the option of settling down in Amritsar, the male family members went to see some of the vacant Muslim houses left behind by those who had fled to Pakistan. Horrified at the condition of some of the houses, which were splattered with blood and the remains of human beings and animals, they decided to go elsewhere. The family went on the move again from one town to another, living in refugee camps, going hungry for days together at times, until they reached Delhi. There they were directed to Malka Ganj, a hilly area in northern Delhi which is opposite the present Hans Raj College of Delhi University. It was an open space, like many shelters in Delhi, where refugees from different parts of West Pakistan came to live. There were about 300 families.

My father and uncles brought big stones from the nearby hillock on a cart and built a small *kutcha* (makeshift) room with mud flooring. My mother started cooking food on wood in the open, just outside that room. Later, she told me that she had wept as she cooked on the first day because she was reminded of the good old days in Panja Sahib where they had a big kitchen and domestic help. However, she thought also of how they had survived the dangers of their journey and thanked God for still being alive. The residents of this colony had to share common makeshift toilets, but they were so few that most of the inhabitants had to go to the fields for defecation. There was no electricity, so everyone had to manage with candlelight or kerosene lamps. To get water, people had to stand in a long queue to fill buckets from the few handpumps installed by the government. We had to sleep on the mud floor, but I remember I was made the most comfortable, being the only child in the family.

We had to rebuild our lives from scratch, just like the more than 5 million Punjabi refugees who had escaped from Pakistan. Most of them settled in Punjab and Delhi, while many others went over to Rajasthan and into distant areas such as the Terai region in Uttar Pradesh (UP), the Chambal Valley and Malwa region of Madhya Pradesh (MP) as well as Bihar, West Bengal, Bombay (now known as Mumbai), Assam and Kerala in search of job opportunities. It was a two-way traffic as many Muslims went over to West Pakistan and many families had suffered retaliatory violence.

From East Pakistan came 2.55 million Hindu refugees. Here, it was a one-way exodus from East Pakistan, unlike in the west, as they were not scattered like refugees from West Pakistan. Most of them settled in West Bengal with others choosing to live in Assam and Tripura. Furthermore, the influx of refugees to West Bengal continued for several decades even after the Partition.

In reconstructing their lives and getting back some level of prosperity,

Punjabi refugees on the western side were most successful due to their hard-working ethic. Everywhere they transcended regional and local barriers—economical, political, social and cultural—to regain their lost wealth.

Many of them got land or homes in lieu of their lands and homes left behind in Pakistan, especially in northern India. The properties allotted to them at their new place were mostly those left behind by people who went to Pakistan from India. My family got neither a house nor land as our only property had consisted of two big houses in Hasan Abdal and three to four *kirana* (grocery) shops as mortgage from people who had taken loans from my rich family. Since these properties were not registered in the family name, we did not get anything in lieu of them.

In hindsight, as my father told me, it turned out to be fortunate that we arrived in Delhi as we could rebuild our lives. I must mention here that my father was and continues to be my only hero, the greatest role model in the world for me. He taught me a lot about life and values and whatever I am today is because of him. With an imposing height of about six feet three inches, he was handsome and slim, always clad in a white *salwar kameez*, and would look very impressive, especially in winter, when he sported the headgear called the *kulla* and *pagri* (turban). *Salwar kameez* was the standard wear for men and women in Pakistan and later for many in India. Even I had a pair that I used to wear on formal occasions. I still have one set which I enjoy wearing sometimes. My father used to wear *murki*s (very small golden earrings) in accordance with a custom in some families that the eldest son had to wear these earrings. So, it is not only today that many males wear earrings as a fashion, just as tattoos were also the style then. Even in 1952, I had a tattoo of my name on my right forearm and still have it.

My father was the eldest of five brothers—three had come with him to Delhi. His fourth brother Madan Lal, immediately younger than him, got married and moved to Rajpura in Punjab where his in-laws had settled down. My grandparents had passed away by then, so my father was like a father to his three younger brothers. He had passed his matriculation examination, one of only three in the region to have this distinction, earning the respect of the community. Fluent in English and Urdu, with beautiful handwriting, he was adept at mathematics. Soon after he passed his matriculation, the British appointed him as a government functionary at a grand salary of Rs 15 per month. He would spend barely three to four rupees where he was posted and send the rest home. When my grandmother passed away, my grandfather had ordered him to leave the job, come home and get married so that there would be a woman in the house to look after the household as even my grandfather's older brother had lost his wife.

Our joint family included my grandfather's elder brother and his two daughters. My father got married, but due to poor medical facilities, his wife died during the delivery of their first child. He married again, this time to my mother who was then just about 14 years of age. My parents saw each other only during their wedding as families used to fix marriages themselves without a single meeting between the boy and girl. I was born after about a decade of my parents' wedding during which period my mother kept praying to all the gods and goddesses to bless her with a child. Finally, her prayers were answered when I came to this planet just before the Second World War ended. She named me Thakur Das as I was considered the gift of God, also called 'Thakur'. Since I didn't like this name, it was changed to my present name, Bhushan Lal (*bhushan* means an ornament).

My mother hailed from Pindigheb, about 114 kilometres from Panja Sahib. She and her elder sister Kaushalya went to school there in those days, a rare feat as the education of girls was usually neglected then, and had studied up to the eighth standard. My maternal grandfather Dewan Chand Sehgal (he had the same name as my paternal grandfather, Dewan Chand Vohra) was a Girdawar, a post above a Patwari and below a Naib Tehsildar, dealing with land and land records and assisting the Naib Tehsildar, who decided revenue cases and performed the duties of an Executive Magistrate apart from acting as an enquiry/supervising officer for issuing important certificates like attestation of mutations, land acquisition cases, demarcation of land and so on. This post exists even today in the Union Territory of Jammu and Kashmir. An equivalent post in Delhi and some other states is that of a Kanungo. As the Girdawar, my grandfather used to visit the courts regularly with land records and was an important person in the society. Whereas my *masi* (my mother's elder sister) was married to a person in Multan Khurd, my mother had moved to Panja Sahib after marriage—by a sheer coincidence both were married into Vohra families. Both the sisters knew how to read and write Gurmukhi, the script of the Punjabi language.

Over the years, my *masi* became deaf, and the two sisters then would communicate by writing in Gurmukhi whenever they met. When I showed a piece of paper with Gurmukhi written on it to my two elder daughters Archana and Sonya, who were then studying in Presentation Convent, they were unable to read the script. In a lighter vein, I asked them who were 'illiterate', they or the two sisters? I explained it was a relative term.

Reverting to the Malka Ganj residence, I vividly remember that one day the roof of our only room fell down and we were roofless for about three days. My mother had fever and I recall her lying down on the ground in the open with a canopy made of a bedsheet by my uncles. I recall that my parents bought me Peshawari chappals, which I proudly wore when we visited the gurudwara near the colony every day and left them outside when we went in for prayers. One day, when I came out, the chappals were missing and I realized somebody had stolen them. In annoyance, I picked up another pair and wore it home, crying all the while. My mother was so furious at my conduct that she slapped me, and pulling me by the ear took me back to the gurudwara to return them. Then she took me inside the gurudwara to the Guru Granth Sahib and made me apologize for my behaviour and take a vow that I would never ever steal again—a lesson which I haven't forgotten till date.

Another incident that I recall vividly is that one morning we saw a coconut along with some flowers and a circular white chalk mark near our house. For us it seemed that somebody had done some kind of *jadu-tona* (a Hindi term for black magic used by people with the evil eye, who were compelled by jealousy or envy) to curse me, a ritualistic practice my mother believed existed. But my father went ahead with showing his contempt as he trampled on the items with his right boot and threw them away. After that such an incident never happened, perhaps because the person who did it noticed my father's action!

Meanwhile, my father and uncles had started looking for jobs. There was the Subzi Mandi, a vegetable and fruit market, nearby where many affluent fruit commission agents from Rawalpindi operated, including someone they considered their brother-in-law. This person was married to their cousin whom they treated as their real sister as they had lived in the same house in Panja Sahib. My father didn't want to ask them for a job, but he somehow managed to get the job of an accountant with another fruit commission agent in the Subzi Mandi. My father was given the task of maintaining the foldable, very long account books called *bahi khata* with bright red cloth covers that were written in the western Punjabi language, called Lande, which had a different script. Later, in addition to his job, my father also tried his own business as a fruit commission agent but was unsuccessful.

While my father got a job, my uncles went to their cousin for help and she got them employed in her husband's firm on the menial job of packing fruits in cartons. Later, two of them, Bhagat Ram and Tilak

Raj, both matriculates, joined the railways as an Assistant Station Master and Goods Clerk, respectively, and left Delhi. They were always kind to me and I owe them a debt of gratitude for looking after me and teaching me many values. The third one, Laik Ram, who had studied only up to the eighth standard, joined the healthcare facility called the Central Government Health Scheme (CGHS) in Delhi as a nursing staff member. He continued to stay in the same house with us in a separate portion in Bharat Nagar where we had moved later on. His children continue to stay in the same colony even now.

In this new refugee colony of Bharat Nagar, one among quite a few that were built in Delhi by the government, there were units of one room and a veranda, about half a room with a huge open window, along with a separate toilet and bathroom at the back with asbestos sheets forming the roof on a plot area of 100 square yards for each unit. There were no boundary walls in some rows. The colony housed about 300 families; each unit was allotted on a rent of Rs 5 per month. We got two units as our family members were more than four in number and that space became our new home. Although my maternal uncles also had two quarters next to us, my maternal grandmother Damodari Devi stayed with us until her death in 1986. I used to call her *Beji*.

To our relief, we finally had a home in a new city in India. The government did its best within the circumstances and despite its financial constraints, which we were grateful for. There was no electricity connection or a flush system and for water requirements, every household installed a handpump in its premises. Piped water connections and electricity came there more than a decade later when I was in the eleventh standard, so until then we managed with kerosene lamps and candles. I used to study at night by the light of these lamps. I recall how thrilled I was on the first day electricity was installed at our house and couldn't stop myself from switching the bulb in the veranda on and off during daytime itself! The flush system took still more time and came about 25 years after the construction of the colony. I discovered what the English commode was when I was in the ninth standard and my uncle Bhagat Ram, who had a job in the railways, took me to the Bhakra Nangal Dam. I had no idea how to use the commode in the guest house, not having seen one before, until my uncle explained it to me. The flush system was installed in our house much after my marriage in 1970, which meant that my wife had to put up with great discomfort as she was used to all the amenities in her affluent home. Later, we moved to a government flat in the Delhi Police colony in Kingsway Camp.

In the absence of a flush system, the human waste was picked up by local sweeper Surat Singh and his family, even his newly married daughter-in-law, every morning from the toilet and carried away on their heads. I was too young to realize that it was below human dignity to carry headloads of excrement, such a shameful practice. After the Untouchability Offences Act was passed by the Indian Parliament in 1955, Surat Singh was made the president of the temple by some enlightened souls in the colony but it was only a symbolic gesture.

Our colony was like a village. It was a rural setting with a fruit orchard at the back of our house. All residents lived like an extended family but belonged to different professions, a few in government and private jobs, others being shopkeepers, workers in the Subzi Mandi, *tonga* (horse-driven carriages) owners, and so on. Everyone knew everyone else. Till date I can remember all the people in the colony very distinctly, and even now, I visit the colony sometimes to meet a few old acquaintances. My father settled comfortably in the new home, cheerfully gardening and solving crosswords in the *Hindustan Times* newspaper on Sundays. Once, he won a grand prize of Rs 25 for solving a crossword correctly! Unfortunately, I haven't picked up these hobbies from him and to top it all, I'm very weak in mathematics, a subject he excelled in, which made him very impatient with me. Now

I tell my grandchildren not to worry if they are weak in mathematics, as it may be in the genes because of me, but I haven't done badly in life.

My father continued with his job till his death in 1976. He was not a religious person in the sense that he never prayed in the temple, unlike my mother, and believed that the best religion is to help the poor and the needy. He would feed the poor, but if a beggar came, he would ask him to work in the household and earn his food. Once, he even gave away his new coat in winter to a person shivering by the roadside though he had bought it after saving money for years.

In those days, except in winter, everyone in the colony would sleep in the open on charpoys just outside their houses on the main *kutcha* (untarred) road. You could also see many charpoys in one row inside the plot areas where there were no boundary walls between houses. A traditional Indian jute-strung poster bed, the charpoy allows extreme coolness as air passes through the ventilation holes in the natural fibre used to string it. Stars and *jugnu*s (fireflies emitting light) could be clearly seen at night in those days, making it a real joy to sleep in the open on moonlit nights. Nature was at its best and in the early morning, we could hear the chirping of birds such as sparrows and parrots and see a variety of snails, snakes and small animals. Trees stood on green open fields just outside the colony. Another sight was rows of the local coal *angithi*s, the traditional braziers used for cooking and heating with the minimum of flames, at the back of the houses.

Playing with friends was our pastime, with the freedom to go to anybody's house for meals at any time of the day, generosity and informality being the hallmarks. Every family treated my friends and me as their own children and even after I joined the police service, many of the *mohalla* (colony) women would fondly call me by name when I visited, making me sit on the charpoy beside them like the good old days, not in the least overawed by my newly acquired status. I liked that.

The asbestos sheet roof gave very little protection from the climate, especially in the extreme heat of summer and the biting cold of winter, but we all got used to it. In summer we used to buy factory ice from the market for an *anna* (four paise) and bring it home in a handkerchief or a small towel. I had never seen a refrigerator until the advent of electricity in our colony in 1960 when our first Sikh tenant who had come from abroad bought a fridge. I was astonished and thrilled to see ice cubes coming straight out of it. There were no vaults to keep jewellery, so it was concealed under the brick floor at different locations by turn in the main room. Nor was there any other furniture except for the charpoys which served also as seats for guests. There was no almirah to keep clothes that were kept in trunks or hung on nails on the walls. The family shared one bar of soap and one towel. Another feature was the rats scurrying around and how we loved to catch them with mousetraps.

A makeshift temple and a gurudwara in the colony were made permanent structures, the common wall between the two speaking of religious harmony. My uncles took an active part in the making of the temple and my mother was a regular visitor there, taking me along always. She performed rituals and kept fasts. Tuesday, the day dedicated to Hanuman, was always a special day for children like me as Hanuman devotees would bring sweet *boondi*s as an offering to the god as *prasad*, which we loved to eat! I learnt most of the *aarti*s or religious rituals performed for different gods and goddesses. However, as I grew out of school, my temple visits were fewer and almost vanished when I joined service. I have remained just an occasional visitor since then.

The colony used to celebrate festivals together with great enthusiasm. *Diya*s (earthen lamps) lit up the colony on Diwali and the local pandit would go to every home to perform the Lakshmi Puja. We used to make our own decorations for the house with colourful paper and I learnt to make a *dola*, a hanging structure with bamboo sticks. The

Lohri festival celebrated the arrival of spring in a big way when *toli*s (small groups) of boys and girls would go to each house to collect Lohri items by singing folk songs like *Sunder mundriye* by the boys and *Hule ni maye hule* by the girls. I was in one such group and would be given a paise or two, or firewood or cow dung cakes. We would distribute the money equally among the group and keep the wood and cow dung cakes to light a bonfire later on the Lohri day that falls on 13 January every year. On Holi, Sardar Niranjan Singh, who lived opposite our house, would ride a donkey with a garland of shoes on it with great fanfare.

A wedding in the colony also meant a celebration for everyone when boys like me made sleeping arrangements by collecting cots and beddings from different houses for the guests, decorated the *shamiana* (the tent venue of the wedding), and participated in the *baraat* (wedding procession) with great fervour. We had quite a few marriages in our house since my uncles got married at the time. Another tradition was presenting the first clothes for a newly born baby—called a *chola*, it was made from cloth belonging to the eldest member of the family as a blessing. During those days, there were a lot of pre- and post-marriage rituals involving both sides of the bride and groom. Nowadays the new generations are either abandoning outdated traditions or foregoing extended ceremonies and choosing shorter versions.

The celebration of my birthday was a regular feature. My mother would take me to the temple in the morning and garland me with marigold flowers. Later, she would call my friends for a lunch of *halwa* and *poori sabzi*, that is, a sweet dish and vegetables with deep-fried wheat bread. However, there were no cameras at home to click photographs, unlike today where we can capture every moment with just a few clicks on our mobile phones!

The *purdah* system was in vogue in the family, a legacy from Islam in the Punjab of earlier days, when the younger married ladies, such as my aunts, would cover their face with a *dupatta* in the presence of senior members like my father who was the eldest in the family. This system is prevalent even today in many societies in India. My father bade farewell to this system when I got married and liberated my aunts also in the process.

The colony was together in times of sorrow too, with most of the residents, except women, joining the funeral processions. Later on, especially those staying nearby, never celebrated any festival or occasion of happiness in their family for one year. I recall that my engagement was a low-key affair because an elderly lady almost next door had passed away.

We had also organized the Ramlila in which I used to play the role of Vibhishan or Kumbhkaran, the brothers of Ravana, the chief villain in the *Ramayan* epic. We used to buy costumes from Chandni Chowk and make swords and bows and arrows of cardboard ourselves. In the first year in Bharat Nagar, when celebrating Dusshera, we made an effigy of Ravana of about 10 feet in height using local resources and our own talent. I was given the lead role in a Tipu Sultan drama (a very poor performance by me!) and that of Rajguru in the drama of Shaheed Bhagat Singh. In another drama, I played an inspector of police, for which I borrowed the khaki uniform of a bus conductor (little did I know then that I would join the police later and wear my own uniform).

We used to play many indigenous games like *gulli-danda* – a popular street sport played with a *gulli* (a small oval-shaped piece of wood) and a *danda* (a long wooden stick), *pithoo* (using seven stones), *stapu*, *kho-kho* and *luka-chhipi* (hide and seek) at no cost. Kabaddi and wrestling were other passions. We also used to play ludo and carrom and enjoyed making paper boats, planes and other items. Kite flying and catching kites cut by other fliers in kite fights was fun. Today, most of these games have vanished and my grandchildren haven't heard of many of them. We also used to play with what nature provided, such as very small snails during the rainy season, and even stole fruits from the orchard near the colony! We used to have fights among friends, sometimes serious, but would make up the next day.

As for medical facilities, there was only our neighbour, Dr Sardari Lal Mehta, who cured ailments by doses of colourful concoctions in small glass bottles with a long vertical white paper label cut in such a way that one could decipher the amount to be taken as a dosage. He would also give medicines in a powder form, wrapped in small white paper packets called *pudiya*. There was no system of prescriptions and medicines being bought from chemists. Doctors close to the Subzi Mandi treated serious illnesses, but if somebody was taken to the hospital, everybody used to think that the patient was on his last legs!

People used to have nourishing meals then. In those days, one visited hospitals only to get major ailments treated and for deliveries. People were generally healthy as they were living in the lap of nature and had simple food at home. Walking was the main activity as there was no other option when going outside the colony for work, school or shopping. Women used to do all domestic work from cleaning the house with brooms, doing *pocha* (mopping the floor), dusting, washing utensils and clothes, cooking, using a *chakki* for grinding wheat, all while sitting on the floor. Most of the women had no access to sanitary napkins or knowledge about the methods of using them. They used pieces of old clothes during menstruation.

Breakfast invariably consisted of a *parantha* (fried wheat bread) with mango pickle, a habit which my grandmother continued till almost her last breath at the age of about 90. The kitchen was in an open space, always a sacred place that could only be entered barefoot. We all used to eat in the kitchen while sitting cross-legged on the floor. We couldn't afford fruits except when prescribed by the doctor and it took me many years to develop a taste for a fruit when I could afford it.

Sometimes we had the luxury of having ripe mangoes which would be put in a water bucket with ice to cool them. During winter, my father used to enjoy brandy with a boiled egg from the market for one *anna*, and I would bring two eggs, one each for both of us.

The vegetables were pesticide-free (organic in today's language) in those good old days. Some seasonal vegetables like cauliflower and *shalgam* (turnips) were dried in the sun so that they could be eaten at any time of the year. *Murabba*, a sweet fruit preserve prepared with spices and sugar, was also made. Mustard oil and Dalda ghee (Dalda was a famous brand name at that time of hydrogenated oil made by Hindustan Vanaspati Manufacturing Co., now Hindustan Unilever Limited) were the medium of cooking, the only two available. Desi ghee was used sparingly for softening *chapati*s. This was available from a shop in Shakti Nagar selling desi ghee of the Keventer brand for Rs 5 a *ser*, a unit of weight like kilogram. Milk was delivered to the homes by buffalo owners in the colony. Once we even had a milk-yielding goat and a cow and I learnt how to milk a cow! In those days, my mother used to make cow dung cakes and dry these in the sun to use as fuel later, a practice which is still prevalent in rural India. The process of drinking tea was a ritual for my mother and grandmother. They would pour tea into a big glass with a narrow base made of *kansa* (a mixed alloy of copper and tin) and then pour it in small portions into *kansa katori*s (bowls), sipping it slowly over a period of time and slurping with enjoyment. Most of our utensils at home were made of *kansa*, which is considered healthy for cooking, but has gone out of fashion these days.

There was neither any system of eating out nor were there any restaurants—we could not afford it anyway. There were no McDonald's, Pizza Hut or other swanky eating joints in those days. At best, we could eat in a *dhaba* (roadside restaurant) when necessary or get *tandoori roti*s made. If we wanted biscuits, we would take flour, ghee, sugar and other ingredients to a nearby small bakery to get them made.

Hygiene meant using a *datun* (a small twig of a neem or kikkar tree) to brush our teeth and toothpaste were not easily available. There was no washbasin in our house when I was a child and it was only 20 years later that my father got one installed when I got married.

For minor ailments, herbal remedies like neem, amla, tulsi, turmeric, lemon, giloy, etc. were used. I still remember the shopkeepers who were always good to everyone. As for haircuts, I can never forget our barber, Tiku Ram. After I joined the police service and was posted as the Additional Superintendent of Police in the Central District of Delhi, Tiku Ram came to my office to seek some help. Unfortunately, the orderly outside, seeing his tattered clothes, would not let him in. The poor fellow waited patiently for a few hours and kept on pleading to the orderly, saying that that he should mention his name to the 'Sahib', and if he wouldn't call him in, he would go away. The orderly took pity on him and as soon as I heard who my visitor was, I promptly called Tiku Ram inside, made him sit comfortably and offered him a cup of tea. I then told the orderly that anybody coming from Bharat Nagar to meet me should not be made to wait.

There was no public transport to commute anywhere from the colony for quite some time. Mostly, people used to go on foot to the 'city', the area around *Ghanta Ghar* (clock tower) on the way to the Subzi Mandi, cutting through Shakti Nagar, a colony that was coming up. My father used to walk to his place of work and back. Some people used *tonga*s while a few privileged ones had bicycles. Once, my family bought an old Raleigh bicycle from an Indian who was based in Africa and had come to visit his sister living in our colony. My father and uncle, the proud owners of this imported cycle, used to flaunt it as the best cycle in the colony! I recall my father jokingly saying that his astrologer's prediction that he would purchase an imported vehicle had come true! After quite some time, an hourly bus service to the Old

Delhi Railway Station was started, which was a big boon. I recall that when I had appeared for the civil services examination in 1966, I used to travel in one of those buses.

After we shifted to Bharat Nagar, I began studying at the nearest school at a distance of about 3 kilometres in Punjabi Basti, located between the *Ghanta Ghar* and Subzi Mandi. When I got admission, *ladoo*s (a popular sweet shaped like a ball) were distributed as was the practice for any celebration in those days. They were also distributed when a child was promoted from one class to another, and on most of happy occasions and functions. I had to walk that distance each way from the first standard itself, along with other students. There were no benches in the classrooms, so we had to sit on the floor, although it was not uncomfortable.

An incident that stands out in my mind is the day I was caught by my father when I played hooky from school. Satvir, my friend from the colony, wasn't interested in attending classes so he would often persuade me to cut classes with him. My father had come to the school for some reason and when he found me missing, he searched nearby places until he saw me in Roshanara Garden with my friend. What a thrashing I got from him that day! He used to keep an eye on me from then onwards and see that I maintained discipline right till I joined the Indian Police Service (IPS).

In school, we wrote on a small rectangular flat wooden board with a handle called a *takhti*, which we had to carry separately as it wouldn't fit into the *basta* (schoolbag). We learnt to write beautifully on it with a bamboo nib, slashed diagonally, after dipping it in *syaahi* (black ink) contained in an inkpot called *dawaat*. The *takhti* had to be cleaned every day with a wet cloth, dried, then coated with *multani mitti* (Fuller's Earth) paste and again dried before use. A writing slate, a kind of mini rectangular blackboard with a wooden frame, was used for mathematics, and we had to write on it with a slate pencil or chalk, then clean it with a wet cloth or slate sponge.

By the time I reached the fourth standard, a school was opened in our colony up to that standard so I was shifted there. Here also there were no benches for students to sit, so I used to take a gunny bag from home to place on the classroom floor. After completing the fourth standard, I was admitted to Birla Higher Secondary School in Kamla Nagar, close to *Ghanta Ghar*, from fifth standard onwards until I passed my Higher Secondary or eleventh standard board examination. It was the best school in that area.

For the first time in my life, I started wearing a school uniform—a white shirt and khaki shorts called *nikkar* in summer and a white shirt, khaki trousers and a blue sweater in winter. The teachers treated us like family members and would even take us home for coaching, if needed. At times, they were strict and as punishment, would often cane us or make us stand on the bench or become a *murga*, where we had to squat like a rooster, loop the arms behind the knees and firmly hold the ears. Having to hold the ears is extremely painful as was caning on the bottoms of erring children. Once, and only once, I was caught copying an answer from another boy's examination paper in the fifth standard, which I foolishly did on the advice of a close friend. My father was called to the school but my mother helped me to get out of the mess as mothers generally do. However, this did not deter me from helping Joginder, my friend whose house was in the same row as mine in Bharat Nagar, to cheat in his board exam. I would write answers for him in the bathroom where he would quickly come and pocket the paper I wrote on.

I was very good in English which we had started learning from the fifth standard. I was made the monitor of the class in the eighth standard because of my adeptness in English though I had fared poorly in maths. My father was astonished at this decision of my class teacher to appoint me as the monitor of the class. Tuitions in our times were only meant for very weak students in some subjects, unlike today when tuitions are taken by almost every student, even the brilliant ones. What a change! While still at school, I had developed the hobby of having pen friends from other countries like the USA, Japan (mostly girls!), and so on. A boy from Pakistan was my pen friend too but an official of the Crime Investigation Department (CID), which tracks such letters, asked my father to dissuade me from having any friend from Pakistan. That was the end of my hobby.

I also visited a posh club for the first time in my life as a young kid with my maternal uncle Anant Ram Sehgal, who was a freelance press photographer. One New Year's Eve, he took me along as his assistant to Roshanara Club, which was close to our colony, in north Delhi. It was a very famous club then. He clicked photographs of well-known personalities partying and dancing. In those days, one bulb was used as a flash for taking a photograph and had to be replaced for the next photo. The cameras had reels of negatives and photos were developed later in a dark room which my uncle had at his house. He would sell these photographs to the celebrities later on. I was overawed by the ambience of the club and the stylish people there.

While at school I got addicted to seeing movies at the Robin Talkies nearby. The front row's ticket would cost two and a half *anna*s (10 paise) and we would enjoy the movie sitting on benches. One of my friends in the school was an expert in jostling past people in the crowd at the ticket counter and buying the tickets quickly. We would watch the first show of each new movie that came to that theatre on the first day (ie., Friday)—a habit that continued while I was in college. By then I had become very fond of watching Hollywood movies although I had to go to New Delhi to cinema halls like Rivoli, Regal and the new Sheila theatre which had come up in Paharganj near the New Delhi Railway Station. I remember seeing hit movies like *El Cid*, *Benhur*, *Sound of Music*, *Spartacus*, *Cleopatra* among others.

I was also fond of reading a popular monthly detective series, *Jasoosi Duniya,* in Hindi by Ibne Safi. Colonel Vinod and Captain Hamid were its main characters. I was fond of reading Hindi novels by Devaki Nandan Khatri, which told stories of magical characters called *aiyar*s (spies) who could transform themselves into any male or female at once! While I was reading these novels, I used to get so engrossed that I could never hear my mother calling me to come to the kitchen for lunch. She would knowingly say, 'So you are reading a novel, not your school books!' The stories of Munshi Prem Chand had made a great impression on me as did *Shakuntala* and *Meghdoot* of Kalidasa. Jonathan Swift's *Gulliver Travels* was another favourite.

I started writing a diary and dreamt of becoming a teacher. A very famous quote impressed and helped me so much that I'm following it even now as it helps me. It is 'Either I'll find my way or make one'. I think I had got it from *Reader's Digest*, which I regularly read. I also did a kind of correspondence course on the Bible.

When I started learning the English alphabet in the fifth standard, my father asked me to start reading the *Hindustan Times* newspaper, which he subscribed to, telling me that anyone who knows English should read newspapers since one can pick up general knowledge that will always stand one in good stead. I acquired an aptitude for both English and general knowledge and that has helped me tremendously. I give the same advice to youngsters, especially those aspiring for the civil services, asking them to read newspapers regularly and seriously.

My other interest was cricket. While still at school, I had become fond of listening to the Test cricket commentary by Devraj Puri and others on radio at the *paan* shops (shops selling aromatics wrapped in betel leaves). Later, I had seen Test matches with Pakistan and Australia at the Feroze Shah Kotla ground in Delhi. The matches used to stretch over six days with a rest day after three days of play. There was neither any one-day nor T20 matches nor any day and night match, all of which were later innovations. About 15 to 20 of us would go to watch a match, taking food and musical instruments like the *dholak* or cymbals borrowed from the temple. We would play these at high decibel levels whenever a boundary was hit by our players or when they got a wicket or when a player of the opponent got out. I remember seeing the Nawab of Pataudi, Ramakant Desai and other famous players from the Indian side; Fazal Mehmood and Hanif Mohammad from Pakistan; and Richie Benaud and Neil Harvey playing for Australia in those matches.

In 1955, my cousin Bimla, the daughter of my *masi* (mother's sister) in Moga, got married and moved to Delhi to live in Subhash Nagar. I had gone to Moga in Punjab with my parents to attend her wedding and it was a great boon for me that she, elder to me by only five-six years, continues to extend her strong support and affection like a real sister. Even though my brother-in-law K.L. Kapoor passed away in 2016, she is still in good health and living with her children.

Bhapaji was a great believer in maintaining relationships. He used to take me and my mother regularly on Sundays or holidays to meet relatives, including his maternal uncle in the Tihar area, even though it wasn't easy to travel by bus in those days. Some of our relatives were quite affluent but always treated us with a lot of respect. I still have contact with some of the new generations of those families. Bhapaji used to say that maintaining relationships means discomfort and having a large heart but it should be done. I try to follow this principle.

Once Tilak Raj, my uncle who was posted in Jaipur where he worked for the railways, had fallen sick. His wife was expecting their first child, so he wrote a letter to Bhapaji, who was like a father to them, explaining the difficult situation and the fact that they had no help. Promptly, my father despatched me to Jaipur. I went by bus and found my own way in the new city to reach my uncle's home. I remember vividly that when I climbed the stairs to reach his flat on the first floor, a woman looked at me and screamed rather excitedly 'How are you here? You didn't tell me that you're coming!' and moved forward to hug me. She was definitely not my aunt. I was confused and tried to stop her by muttering, 'Where does Mr Tilak Raj stay? I have come to meet him.' Now it was her turn to get confused. She said, 'He is our neighbour here but what do you have to do with him?' I told her that he was my uncle. In short, she had mistaken me for someone else as my face resembled someone in their family. That facial resemblance to others is a recurring episode in my life. I have often experienced people mistaking me for someone else. It has happened at airports, parks, functions, and I always enjoy such encounters.

Since every school student wanted to take science in those days from the ninth standard onwards to become an engineer or doctor, I was also forced to take it, which turned out to be a disaster. Physics, chemistry and mathematics were my sworn enemies, so I fared poorly in the final exams in 1960. In those days, getting a first division with 60 per cent and above was a rarity and going for tuition was a blot. I barely managed to pass and that too with a compartment in physics (which meant that I had failed in the subject but was given the option to reappear for the exam without repeating the academic year). But, as I keep telling my grandchildren, that alone doesn't mean that success becomes elusive. Though a mediocre student, I was good at outdoor activities in school and would play all sports, including football, volleyball, basketball and cricket, something that is still part of my life. We used to go for cycling on hired bicycles, play kabaddi and wrestle. I was also a part of the school band to play the flute. With great pleasure, I visited the school a few years ago along with my wife and daughter Manika to give shoes, sweaters and other items to some of the needy children.

Incidentally, there were quite a few criminals also in the colony, including a notorious smuggler. I used to be teased about it by Pandit

Lal Chand, the Deputy Superintendent of Police (DSP) of the Chandni Chowk area when I was his boss in the North District in Delhi. He once said, 'Sir, how come an IPS officer has emerged from a colony of criminals?' As it happens, our colony was in the jurisdiction of the North District in which I was posted. It was indeed remarkable to get a home posting after joining the IPS and being allotted the Union Territory (UT) cadre.

In 1960, when I completed my Higher Secondary, that is, the eleventh standard (there was no 10+2 system then), India had completed 13 years of independence. We had adopted a Constitution on the British model on 26 January 1950. Democracy was ushered in though many were sceptical about its continuance in a land where illiteracy was rampant. Fortunately, it has stood the test of time, which is no mean achievement. India is a multilingual, multireligious, multicultural nation—a tremendous geographical entity. Sardar Patel, the Deputy Prime Minister and the Home Minister, had then embarked upon the huge task before the new government—unifying India by bringing into its fold over 562 princely states that were part of the erstwhile British-ruled provinces. The Congress Party had won the general elections in 1952 and 1957 and the government was led by Jawaharlal Nehru. He adopted the system of Five-Year Plans based on the USSR model for economic development with a prominent role for the state as heavy investments were required. He was also one of the founders of the Non-Aligned Movement as India didn't want to join either the USA or USSR camp.

However, the biggest challenge was to feed people—food production was lagging, so India had to depend on the USA for food supplies under Public Law 480 (PL-480) from 1954 against rupee payments. It was said that India lived a 'ship-to-mouth' existence in those days. Later, India realized its mistake when the USA temporarily suspended sending food grains in the 1960s due to some political differences and

India faced a back-to-back drought. It was then that the government decided to develop its own agriculture. As a result, in 1966, India imported 18,000 tonnes of newly developed high-yielding varieties of wheat from Mexico, which was put to use by Punjab farmers and those of the adjoining areas, encouraged by incentives and subsidies. This development led to the Green Revolution. India today not only produces enough food for its increased population of about 130 crore but also has enough to export—a matter of great pride for us. Hats off to the agricultural scientists and farmers of the country!

In 1956, the States Reorganization Act was passed for the reorganization of the states on linguistic basis. Delhi, which was earlier a Chief Commissioner's province, became a Union Territory (UT) ruled directly by the Centre. Politically, it was a battleground between the Congress and Bharatiya Jana Sangh (the predecessor of the Bharatiya Janata Party, BJP). Chaudhary Brahm Prakash of the Congress and Balraj Madhok, Kedar Nath Sahni, and L.K. Advani of the Bharatiya Jana Sangh were the main leaders, apart from many others. Both the parties shared the honours at the hustings. It was a great pleasure to listen to Atal Bihari Vajpayee in election meetings as he was a great orator. The one I remember distinctively was in Ajmal Khan Park in Karol Bagh in Delhi where I was a part of a huge crowd that had gathered to listen to him. Later, as an IPS officer, I had a couple of personal encounters with him.

Chapter 2

College and Employment

I was excited about joining a college after school, expecting much less discipline and lots of freedom, unlike in school. I decided to go in for a Faculty of Science (F.Sc.) degree (now dispensed with as a college degree) from Hindu College, Sonipat, just outside Delhi in Punjab then (now in Haryana). The college was just beside the railway station, there so I would commute by train with my friends to Sonipat every day. My mother had to pawn her jewellery to meet my admission fee and other expenses. She was perhaps not aware that she had a useless son. For me, it was great fun to go to college but I took no interest in studies and would regularly bunk classes. Spending time with friends in canteens or other joints in between college hours had its own charm. Instead of attending lectures, I would see movies regularly at Robin Talkies with my school friend Jagat Sarup, who was my constant partner in this crime. Even though physics and chemistry were my subjects, I never did any work in the laboratory. The result, as expected, was that I failed the examination to the utter dismay of my parents. But I was so irresponsible that this outcome did not affect me at all as I didn't realize the gravity of the situation.

Then my father decided to put me in a college in Delhi to do a Bachelor of Arts (BA) course as I was unfit for science subjects. Through a connection, Professor N.D. Kapoor, he got me admitted in Hans Raj College, but in those days, it was easy to get admission in colleges in Delhi as marks obtained in the Higher Secondary examination was hardly a criterion. When I filled up the form, I chose BA (Hons.) English since that was the subject I thought I was good at. However, I switched my subject to economics on the advice of Professor Kapoor, who said a degree in economics would have more scope in the employment market. So, I landed up in the Economics (Hons.) class with renowned Professors J.D. Khatri of economic theory and G.D. Jangid of Indian economy apart from other professors. Incidentally, the monthly college fee was Rs 15 and I was entitled to a 50 per cent concession since I was a refugee.

On the first day of college, I sported a smart haircut and wore specially stitched black trousers, with a white shirt (in those days readymade clothes were not available), and cycled to college. It was a festive atmosphere. The then principal, Shri Shanti Narayan, a renowned mathematician, addressed the new students, welcoming them to the college. It was a boys' college only with no girls around, which was a bit of disappointment but I took it in my stride. Some ragging of freshers took place for two days or so, but then quietened. My class consisted of about 30 students, some of whom did exceptionally well later on.

Suhas Laxman Ketkar, who got a first division in the final examination, became a renowned economist with the United Nations (UN), Anil Chaudhary joined the Bharat Ram Group in a senior position, Raghavan (I don't recall his full name) became a chartered accountant, and so on. We also had Promod Mahajan, son of Chief Justice of India Mehar Chand Mahajan, as a classmate. My close friend in the class was P.S. Natarajan and another friend was Darshan Lal Sachdeva, the Assistant Librarian of the college library, a gem of a person who continues to be my benefactor and a dear friend even now.

When I started studying economics, I became a serious and responsible student, as I found the subject very interesting. Professors Khatri and Jangid had written excellent books on economic theory and Indian economy, respectively, which were very useful.

However, studying in college did not mean only work. We liked playing pranks such as when we placed firecrackers in the class in such a way that they exploded as soon as the professor's lecture started. It was to scare away a new professor, Ranga Rao. Sahib Ram Khera, a bus conductor, was also our classmate. He used to miss classes due to his job, so to help him out, my friends and I would say 'present' when his name was called out. Once I was caught doing so in the Hindi class, an optional subject, but somehow managed to convince the professor that I was indeed Khera!

When there was a demonstration at an embassy in Chanakyapuri, I joined the crowd just to have some fun and broke some flower pots in the compound of the embassy. At once, we were rounded up and dragged to the police station nearby, but then let off after being reprimanded.

I also contested elections to the college Parliament twice and got publicity handouts printed in Kamla Nagar, a market near the university. On both occasions I won and during my second tenure, was made the Education Minister, but I resigned in protest as I had been promised the Home Ministry by the college's Prime Minister. Incidentally, it was for the first time that I had a scooter ride sitting on the pillion of the prime ministerial candidate who had dropped me home once during those days of elections.

When I was in college, China invaded India in Arunachal Pradesh in the North-East on 20 October 1962, which resulted in a humiliating defeat for India. After about a month of the war and occupying a large stretches of our territory, China unilaterally announced a ceasefire.

Prime Minister Jawaharlal Nehru, an idealistic person, thought that China would not attack India as the Sino-Indian agreement of 1954 had cemented the *Panchsheel* or the Five Principles of Peaceful Co-existence between the two countries and '*Hindi–Chini Bhai Bhai*' was a popular slogan. China's Prime Minister had also been given a big welcome when he visited India earlier. So most people felt that China had stabbed us in the back. The war demoralized Nehru and affected his health. I saw him in person just once when he addressed the National Cadet Corps (NCC) cadets on our college ground. I saw him from far away as I was in a queue at quite a distance. I was in my NCC uniform as I had joined the NCC out of patriotic fervour, but it had also been made compulsory at that time for college students to be part of it.

Our border dispute with China continues till date. Our latest skirmish with it was in May 2020 and India gave a good account of itself, showing it is no longer weak. In fact, China has withdrawn from some areas and there is a stalemate elsewhere.

The habit of seeing a film on the day of its release, ie., Friday, which I had acquired in school and later while studying in Sonipat, continued. Later in life I lost interest in films, but now, after retirement, I do occasionally see a movie at the theatre.

For the first time in my life, I learnt, perhaps subconsciously, that I needed a lot of self-improvement and had to get rid of my inferiority complex and shyness. I slowly started working towards self-improvement in mannerisms and attitudes. I even started going to restaurants nearby in Kamla Nagar to observe, for example, how to eat hotdogs and how cutlery was used. I tasted coffee for the first time. When in the ninth standard, I became adept at fixing a necktie, which I learnt from Sardar Ajit Singh in Bharat Nagar, who always wore a tie as he was working as an Upper Division Clerk (UDC) in a government office. I sheepishly told him that I wanted to learn how to tie the knot of the necktie, so he taught me and even gave me a bright red tie.

This habit of trying to improve myself has stayed with me since my college days and continues even now, though I'm now beyond 78 years. I may have thought that I was good at English but I was wrong. My vocabulary and pronunciation are poor as a high level of teaching English did not exist in my school. Even now, I consult the dictionary frequently and have constantly learned from my children who have been educated in convents, unlike me.

I had not heard of the prime civil services, such as the Indian Administrative Service (IAS) and IPS, till I was in the second year of college. I came to know about them by chance. One day when I went to the house of Sudesh, my friend in Bharat Nagar, he proudly showed me some photographs of his elder brother, Ved Prakash Kapur, who was wearing a smart suit with a tie and standing in a group photograph with others who were similarly dressed. He told me that his brother had become a police officer and the photographs were from the Mussoorie Academy where these officers were trained. I couldn't comprehend what he meant, but was impressed in a big way. Sometime later he told me that his brother was posted at Jhansi in UP and was getting married there. He invited me and a few other friends of the colony to join the celebrations. At the Jhansi Junction Railway Station (now renamed as Virangana Laxmibai Railway Station), we were taken to his brother's bungalow in police jeeps, and we marvelled at the huge residence, where orderlies, security guards and policemen saluted him. The *baraat* (bridegroom's procession) went to Bhopal from there and we attended a grand reception hosted by the bride's father who was a Chief Engineer in MP. The return of the marriage party along with the bride to Jhansi was again a grand affair, and for the first time I witnessed a welcome by a grand police band at the railway station. Perhaps this was the inspiration for the beginning of my aspirations to become an IPS officer. Ved Bhapaji was then the

Assistant Superintendent of Police (ASP). He was 1961 batch of IPS and retired as DGP of UP.

I understood then what the status of the IPS was and began to long to join it. I resolved to find out about the procedure necessary to get into the service and when I did, I discovered that one had to appear in a very tough competitive examination to qualify for the IAS and IPS, which only one per cent of candidates could pass. However, it was still only a thought at this stage.

While I was in college, my reading habit continued. I read many books including Nehru's *Discovery of India*, Mahatma Gandhi's *My Experiments with Truth*, Lala Har Dayal's *Hints for Self-Culture* and many autobiographies of successful people. Earlier, I would borrow books from the Delhi Public Library near the Old Delhi Railway Station, which widened my horizon and world view further. I read quite a bit of literature on Communism and became a Leftist in thought as many young men do. However, over the years, this leaning went away when I saw more of the world.

In college, there used to be only one final examination of the university at the end of three years and I had to appear in eight papers. There was no yearly university exam or semester system exams as is the case now.

By the time I entered the final year, I began my search for a job so that I could work soon after graduation. For those of us living in the refugee colony of Bharat Nagar, managing to get the job of a clerk in the government was the ultimate equivalent of becoming even a Governor! I learnt how to type, a skill required for the post of a clerk. My typing school was in Shakti Nagar where I would go after college. It took me a month or two to learn the basics, but I was always prone to committing mistakes and not being fast enough. I could never type efficiently and I found it difficult to attain the required accuracy and speed. Fortunately, in those days, government departments were flexible enough to also hire candidates subject to the condition that the required standards would be met within six months of joining.

When I applied for the post of a Lower Division Clerk (LDC) in the Municipal Corporation of Delhi (MCD), I failed as expected in the typing test, but was given the job on the condition that I would qualify after passing the typing test within six months. Since I wasn't sure that I would do so, I slept over that appointment letter for some time, hoping that something else would come to me. I also thought of becoming an X-ray technician or a flight purser, but my father shot down these ideas. Ashok Chawla, who had later come to the colony, became my lifelong friend during one of the typing tests for a job when we both happened to go together after hiring the typewriter from the same shop. Unfortunately, we lost him to Covid in 2021. Although less than normal efficiency did not get me a job, I'm using the basic skill of typing now on computer keyboards and mobiles, which is a blessing. To my surprise, I'm much faster than many people and this makes me believe that whatever one takes the trouble to learn never goes waste and can come in handy later. Meanwhile, the third and final year was coming to an end and my last shot was to appear for the clerk's grade examination held by the Union Service Public Commission (UPSC) annually.

Since my final exams were close by, I forgot for the time being about getting a job and instead, concentrated on my studies because my future depended on the results. Surprisingly, I became studious and responsible. Personally I felt I did well in the exams and got sixth rank in the class with 49 per cent, which was still a third division as 50 per cent and above earned one a second division and above 60 per cent first division. Only one student in my class got that while four had got the second division—a rarity in those days.

As I was relaxing after the exams, I hit a jackpot. I cleared the clerk's grade competition held by the UPSC in the first week of May 1964 before the graduation results came in and was posted as a LDC in the Ministry of Rehabilitation located in Jaisalmer House near India Gate. It was a matter of great joy and celebration at home and in the colony and our social status went up by quite a few notches. It was on 27 May 1964, a very hot day, when I got ready to go to my new office but not before my mother carried out her customary ritual on any important occasion, by feeding me curd and sugar. I first cycled to North Block because I had no clue about where Jaisalmer House was, refuelling myself en route with *lassi* (buttermilk). Then I saw a huge crowd outside North Block which is near Ram Manohar Lohia Hospital (then called Willingdon Hospital) and on inquiring, got to know that Prime Minister Jawaharlal Nehru had died. I had to go back home as I was told that all the Central government offices would be closed for two days to mourn his death.

Two days later, I peddled to Jaisalmer House, almost an hour's journey from Bharat Nagar. Being young and full of enthusiasm, I was delighted to see my new office in the Dandakaranya section on the ground floor of the building. As luck would have it, in a sheer coincidence about 38 years later in July 2002, my office was again in Jaisalmer House, this time on the first floor, when I became the Director General of Civil Defence. From the lowest position in the government hierarchy, I was reposted back to the same building in the highest position equivalent to a Secretary in Government of India. My life took full circle, taking me 38 years to climb just 36 stairs! This is the reason why the subtitle of this autobiography is *From and To Jaisalmer House*.

Strangely, all important landmarks in my life have come in the month of May—whether it was my first job, my UPSC interview for the IAS, my marriage, most of my transfers and promotions, and many other important events. So each year I eagerly look forward to May with anticipation, hoping it'll be lucky for me.

Dina Nath Hasija was my Section Officer when I joined the ministry. He was a man in his fifties, portly, handsome and a gentleman. I was posted as a receipt and despatch clerk. My job was to enter in a register the number and subject of each file received and sent along with the date, a simple task in which I was trained by Hasija himself. When the clock struck 11 a.m. on the first day, UDC Tilak Raj Malik got up from his seat. Others followed him and he signalled to me to accompany them too. We all went to the canteen for a cup of tea and *pakoras* (Indian snacks) as a mid-morning break. There he gave me a sermon, saying, 'Look, Bhushan, my advice to you is to take your job lightly. Every day we all have a cup of tea together at 11 a.m. and 3.30 p.m. so you must always join us and relax for the rest of the day. You can even go out of the office whenever you feel like. You'll take 16 years to get your first promotion and become a UDC, which I'm now. So don't work hard!' I meekly nodded. I was learning the ropes!

Following his advice, I began walking out of the section for no rhyme or reason, just to loiter around. After some days, Hasija asked me to stay back after office hours. When all the others left, he called me over and counselled me. Apparently, he had seen me leaving the office room frequently for no reason and going with the other crowd twice for a cup of tea every day. He told me that I was a young boy and a whole life's career was before me; therefore, I should not listen to people like Malik, but learn to be sincere and hard-working. He told me that diligence would pay dividends in the long run and that I should strive to improve my career prospects.

About 23 years later in 1987, when I was the Deputy Inspector General (DIG) (Range) in New Delhi in the Central Reserve Police Force (CRPF), Hasija came to meet me. He had settled in Canada by then after his retirement as his children had migrated there. He was on a visit to Delhi and managed to find out where I was, even though there were no mobiles or Facebook in those days. I was delighted to meet him and thanked him for his advice years ago which helped me in furthering my career.

I can never forget the day when I received Rs 166 in brand new notes as my first salary. I was so delighted. When I handed over the salary to my mother, she kissed me and even the notes! She took me to the temple to thank the Lord for his kindness and for enabling me to add to the family income. I have an annoying habit of telling my grandchildren repeatedly about the amount of my first salary. It must be so boring for them to hear it time and again but I can't help it in spite of my wife's warnings.

Just before beginning my first job, I had also appeared in two written competitions for the post of UDC, each conducted by the State Trading Corporation (STC) and the Minerals and Metals Trading Corporation (MMTC). About 3,000 candidates each had appeared for 15 vacancies in each organization. I got into the first 15 in both the examinations and got the third rank in the MMTC exam. Somehow, I was always successful at clearing competitions perhaps because I was comparatively good in English and general knowledge due to my habit of reading the *Hindustan Times* regularly. Just when I had completed about two months in the Ministry of Rehabilitation, I got the offer of an appointment from the MMTC as a UDC. Its office was located in *The Indian Express* building at Bahadur Shah Zafar Marg between Delhi Gate and ITO. It was a big promotion for me, so I resigned from my job and moved on to work as a UDC with a higher salary of Rs 220 per month in July 1964.

Meanwhile, Lal Bahadur Shastri of the Congress had succeeded Jawaharlal Nehru and became the Prime Minister of India. Indira Gandhi, the daughter of Nehru, was inducted as the Minister of Information and Broadcasting. A person with a short height but big stature in his professional life, Shastri had a formidable reputation as a person of integrity. He was a leader worthy of respect and admiration.

Earlier, he had resigned as the Minister of Railways and Transport in 1956, owning moral responsibility for a train disaster in Ariyalur in Tamil Nadu in which 144 people had lost their lives. By doing so, he set a high benchmark for politicians. In Indian politics, resigning on moral grounds is a rare phenomenon.

In the MMTC, I was posted to the accounts department, which was really bad luck for me as maths and accounts are my sworn enemies. To cap this, I got not one but two bad bosses, Aggarwal and Gandhi. The latter was particularly inimical towards me, at least that was what I thought, and I ran into rough weather from the word go. My work related to the preparation of papers and bills of lading for ships carrying Indian goods from ports to other countries. Since I didn't like the work, I was prone to committing mistakes. The only thing that I liked—and miss even now—was that I had travelled in a chauffeur-driven Mercedes car to Parliament Street to hand over the bills to the Ministry of Shipping. The chauffeur, in a smart white uniform, would open doors for me and salute me elegantly. It was a big thing in 1964.

Gandhi would often pull me up for my poor and casual work. One day, he caught me napping in my chair and reprimanded me, saying, 'You are behaving as if you're a big officer.' I retorted indignantly, 'Actually, I *will* become a big officer. These are temporary days.' He laughed at me mockingly and went away.

Meanwhile, I also attended evening classes in the Arts Faculty of Delhi University, aiming for a Master of Arts (MA) degree in economics. This meant that I had to cycle about 25 kilometres every day, in the morning from Bharat Nagar to the Indian Express building and in the evening from there to the university. I would reach home by about 10 p.m.

Soon I got an opportunity to escape from the mess of the accounts department. Since my friend Gyan of Bharat Nagar was getting married and the marriage party was to go to Dehradun, I applied for three days' leave, but my request was promptly refused by Gandhi. Back home in the evening, I told Gyan what had happened. He came up with a solution as he was assisting his father, who was a commission agent in Subzi Mandi, dealing with vegetables and making good money. He told me to resign and offered to pay my full salary till I got another job. Emboldened, I went to the office the next day and asked for leave verbally again, but Gandhi got so angry and abusive that I wrote my resignation letter there and then and handed it over to him. He was shocked but didn't say anything. My colleagues tried to persuade me to take it back but I was adamant. At home in the evening, I told my mother about the whole thing. She was very upset but keeping calm, she said, 'People don't get government jobs and here you have resigned foolishly. What if you don't attend the wedding? I won't tell your father about this as it will enrage him. Go to office in the morning and take your resignation back.' I was in a bind. Mentally stressed, I reached office next morning.

To my surprise, a peon came up to me and said that the higher authority, Mrs I. Indira, an officer of the Indian Audit and Accounts Service, on deputation to the MMTC, had summoned me. I guessed that it must be regarding my resignation as my colleague had informed me that my resignation had been sent to her by Gandhi. Nervous, as I was entering the room of a senior officer for the first time in my life, I wished her almost in a whisper. She made me comfortable, asking me to sit on the chair across her, and then politely asked me the reason for my resignation. I told her the truth – about the wedding and also that I wanted to be free from Gandhi and the accounts branch as I was unfit for it, apart from being treated badly. She picked up my resignation letter, tore it into pieces and threw it into the dustbin. She told me that my leave was granted. I heaved a sigh of relief, especially happy when she said I would be posted in another department when I returned. For me, it was as if I got a second life.

As I turned to leave, she called me back again and advised me to try for the civil services, saying she was confident that I could make it. I don't know what she saw in me and why she thought I was capable of cracking the civil services examination despite the intense competition it meant. I thanked her for her kindness and I have always remained indebted to her for her help, advice and encouragement.

I went with the marriage party along with Sudesh and some other friends to Dehradun. When we had some spare time, we went to bathe in a spring at Sahastradhara, about 15 kilometres from Dehradun town, which abounds in waterfalls, caves and lush greenery. I was keen to go to Mussoorie, the famous hill station only 35 kilometres from Dehradun, but couldn't as there was no time. But the longing remained and God fulfilled that wish some years later when I went to Mussoorie for quite a few months to attend the foundational course in the Lal Bahadur Shastri Academy of Administration as an IPS officer.

I had also picked up more friends during that period, thanks to Ashok Chawla, my dear friend, who had joined the Reserve Bank of India (RBI). He introduced me to his colleagues, P.L. Suri, P.K. Gupta and S.K. Sood, who became my friends too. I also found a lifelong friend in B.R. Lall from the RBI whom I met at Mount Abu later as my batchmate in the IPS. He passed away some years ago.

After returning from Dehradun, I was posted to another department which had nothing to do with accounts. A.K. Gopalan, who was quite formal but a good man, was the Section Officer there. I made good friends in the section, out of whom L.D. Gauba and P.C. Kumar continue to be my friends till date. Gulshan, a girl in the branch, was affectionate like a sister and we were in touch for a long time. There were other seniors who were very kind, so life became good. I also had a crush on a girl but she took no interest in me. I confided in Gulshan who was willing to take it forward and help me, but I declined, feeling that furthering my career was more important than romance and marriage. I wanted to move upwards from my position and do well. Two of my section mates took me for a beer party one day in Daryaganj. It was the first time that I drank beer. I didn't like the taste but kind of felt proud that I was growing up!

I had, in the meanwhile, appeared for the Assistant Grade competition held by the UPSC for a rank just below a Section Officer but above the UDC. These days the Assistants are called Assistant Section Officers. My father was the spirit behind my efforts to improve my career, always egging me on to strive further. He would get the forms, copy these by hand as there were no photocopiers then and guide me by listing important questions. However, there was a big catch in the Assistant Grade exam. There was a paper on mathematics, basic arithmetic that was bound to be my Waterloo.

Since Ashok Chawla, my friend, was good at mathematics, my father asked him to take leave for a few days and coach me. He obliged and I tried my best to learn, with some success. I cleared that competition, ranking 37th in the all-India merit list. In maths I scored a glorious 86 out of 100. I thought that the UPSC had given these marks by mistake but I wasn't bothered. At least I had qualified—and so well too! I moved to the Railway Board on yet another promotion in September 1965 as an Assistant. My salary in the new job was almost Rs 400 per month, a big jump again. Of course, the value of money those days was also much more. By this time, my cousin Kamlesh—from Rajpura, Punjab, and the son of my uncle Madan Lal—had settled in Delhi. He was working with the railways and has been a big source of strength to me. Unfortunately, I lost him recently.

In the Railway Board, I was posted again to a section that had uninteresting work and a Section Officer who was more depressing than the work. We were a big batch of newly appointed assistants, three of whom became very good friends—M.M.K. Katial, Balbir Singh and Avinash Makani. We foursome had great fun in the

Railway Board office, which was in Rail Bhawan near Parliament House. In the canteen, we used to pick up a tray of *dosa*s every day and polish them off. Balbir became the Railways National Champion in badminton, but when he tried to teach us, Makani would find fault with every stroke played by Balbir because he could not return even one! I did the same. We, therefore, appointed Makani as our *Kaptan* (Captain). He continues to hold that position even today. Among all the four, Katial had the most colourful personality and was well-read. He was talented, being a master of music and a tuneful singer apart from playing instruments like the harmonium and flute.

I managed to get out of the section with the help of friends and got posted to another section on the third floor of the Railway Bhawan. This room was in a corner at the back of the building, and from the window, I could see Parliament House. Dwarka Das, my new Section Officer, was a jolly good fellow. He used to stammer but still would talk a lot. In that very room, I met J.D. Kapoor, a pleasant and hard-working person. He later joined the judiciary and rose to become a judge of the Delhi High Court. We have been in touch.

At the time I shifted from the MMTC to the Railway Board, the 1965 war between India and Pakistan was fought in September 1965. This was a culmination of skirmishes that had taken place between India and Pakistan since April that year. The conflict began following Pakistan's Operation Gibraltar, which was designed to infiltrate forces into Jammu and Kashmir (J&K) to precipitate an insurgency against India by the Kashmiris. This did not happen.

India retaliated by launching a full-scale military attack on the Punjab side of West Pakistan. The 17-day war caused thousands of casualties on both sides. The war witnessed the largest engagement of armoured vehicles and the largest tank battle since the Second World War. The air forces of the two countries also got involved, carrying out aerial combat operations against each other. Both countries seized territories of each other with India capturing more, including fertile land of Punjab on the Pakistani side. India won the war decisively and it ended after a ceasefire was declared by the UN following the Tashkent Declaration at the intervention of the USSR (Union of Soviet Socialist Republics) and the USA. Prime Minister Shastri and Pakistan President Ayub Khan signed the historic pact in the presence of USSR Prime Minister Alexei N. Kosygin in Tashkent, the capital of Uzbekistan.

The very next day on 11 January 1966, Shastri mysteriously died in Tashkent. It was said that he died of a cardiac arrest but many among Shastri's close relatives and supporters alleged foul play. Shastri had already earned fame and popularity by his slogan '*Jai Jawan Jai Kisan*' ('Hail the Soldier, Hail the Farmer') and by ordering the Indian army to attack Pakistan from the Punjab side and to move to Lahore. His sudden demise paved the way for Mrs Indira Gandhi, who was the Minister of Information and Broadcasting, to become the next Prime Minister of India, chosen by the ruling Congress Party.

I used to go to Rail Bhawan by changing two buses and doing the same on my return. In the evening, since the bus route was via Connaught Place, Makani and I would usually go for coffee to a restaurant above Regal Cinema. Makani was very fond of consuming almost all the sugar cubes served along with the two cups of coffee. I also used to take him to *The Indian Express* building so that he could teach mathematics to Gauba, my friend in the MMTC there, who was doing higher studies by correspondence and needed help in mathematics. I would play table tennis while Makani taught Gauba.

As for my studies, I could not pass my MA Economics examination as my father fell seriously sick with severe diarrhoea and vomiting during the examination days. I had to attend to him the whole night and couldn't write my paper the next day.

However, buoyed by my success in the competitions, and encouraged by my father, I started thinking of appearing for the IAS examination the next year, 1966. I suggested that all my friends in the Railway Board should appear in this examination, but they replied with a big 'No', stating it was a very difficult competition. Anyway, I decided to go ahead. The best part of this exam of the UPSC is that there is no minimum percentage of marks required before and after graduation. One just has to be a graduate. So even though my academic record was poor, I was eligible to appear. Dwarka Das, my Section Officer, was very supportive. Due to financial reasons, I couldn't afford to take long leave without pay to prepare. He, however, permitted me to leave office for studies after marking my attendance on most days and making me do only essential work.

I had chosen geography, international law and European history in addition to economics as my subjects for the examination. I still recall that along with Gauba, my friend in the MMTC, I went to a bookshop in Gole Market to buy books on these subjects to study. I bought just two books, one by M.K. Tandon on international law and the other by L. Mukherjee on European history, and read only these. Since economics was my subject for my BA, and I was also attending evening classes for an MA in economics, I had enough notes. But still I had to prepare a lot for English, writing essays, and so on. There was no system of a preliminary examination first to be followed by the main examination to be further followed by a personality test as there is at present. There was only one written examination consisting of eight papers, including two advanced papers followed by the interview if the candidate cleared the written examination.

There was only one institute, Rau's IAS Study Circle, in Connaught Place that offered coaching for preparations for the IAS. The great Mr Rau was a one-man army running a very successful show and every year, many students coached by him were qualifying in the examination, including quite a few in the top ten. When I went to him for coaching, he refused to admit me after talking to me, considering me an undeserving candidate. That demoralized me but I decided to find my own way. I used to go to a small library next to the main library near the Arts Faculty and spend almost the whole day there reading whenever possible. At home also, I used to slog quite a bit. In office, after marking my attendance, I used to go to the lawns near the Boat Club with my study material. I was very keen to clear the exam and somewhat hopeful and confident too about my success. However, there was one big stumbling block. In the paper on English every year, a poem was given for critical appreciation and I could never understand these poems in English. This could be my Waterloo but I couldn't help it.

During 1966, when I was preparing for the IAS examination, Haryana state was created by bifurcating Punjab on 1 November 1966 on a linguistic basis consisting of Hindi-speaking areas. General elections were also held in India in February 1967. These were landmark elections since the Congress Party returned to power with much less majority, only 284 seats out of 542 seats, for the first time and formed the government with support from some Left parties and others. Indira Gandhi was made the Prime Minister. This was also the last time that the Lok Sabha and Assembly elections were held simultaneously.

The Congress lost power in many states and a coalition of parties calling themselves the Samyukt Vidhayak Dal (SVD) formed governments in many states including UP, Bihar, Rajasthan, Punjab, West Bengal, Orissa, Madras and Kerala. In many states in the North where the Congress had won narrow victories, its members defected to the other parties and it was replaced by the SVD as ruling party. The parties in the SVD were the Jana Sangh, Socialists, Swatantra Party, some local parties and defectors from the Congress. It was a watershed event leading to more changes in Indian politics later on.

Our branch was put on election duty to manage a polling booth in the Karol Bagh area of Delhi with Dwarka Das in the lead. Earlier, I had worked once as a polling agent of the Bharatiya Jana Sangh in one of the local elections and this was my second experience of elections in a different role.

Reverting to my exams, luckily for me there was no poem in the 1966 IAS exam. Instead, there were two paragraphs, one each by Lord Macaulay and Raja Ram Mohan Roy, both supporting learning of English by Indians but for different reasons. We had to explain the rationale behind their recommendations. I was delighted and did justice to the question. That day I was confident that I would qualify as I had done fairly well in other papers also.

And I did pass the written examination in the very first attempt. The highlight was that I got 76 per cent in the advance paper of Indian economy, even though I had only read the book of my erstwhile college's Professor Jangid, updating myself on the Indian economy from the newspapers. I got 60 per cent in both international law and European history. I was called for the interview or the personality test as they called it. I went to Rau's IAS Study Circle again for coaching for the interview and this time Rau took me in because the raw material had become better! After a few days, he asked me whether I had a dark-coloured lounge suit because I had to wear one on the day of the interview. It was to be held in the month of May in 1967 when Delhi is very hot.

I didn't own a coat, so I told my father about Mr Rau's advice. A year earlier, he had bought a warm blue cloth for me from a shop in Chandni Chowk, which was stitched into pants. We both went to that shop next day in the hope that the same cloth may be available so we could get a coat stitched. We were lucky—the same cloth was right there and the suit could be made!

Reverting to Rau, my first mock interview with him and other students who formed a panel with him was a total disaster. I became nervous and couldn't answer many questions. Not giving up on me, he coached me thoroughly. As a part of my preparation, I had gone around Delhi in the tourist bus of the government with a guide so that I could get familiar with various historical and important locations in Delhi as questions about Delhi were expected. One ritual Rau insisted on was that on the day of the interview, each of his students had to go to him in the morning on the way to the UPSC. He wanted to update us on the latest news and clarify any last-minute questions. Afterwards, the candidate had to meet him to brief him about the interview so that he would make his assessment about the chances of success, including perhaps the likely rank by merit. He was very hard-working and an institution by himself. God bless his soul!

On the D-day, I also went to him in the morning and then left for the UPSC. My interview was in the forenoon. I didn't do that well in the interview but was still confident about getting through in the final list. In another instance of my life coming full circle, I was on this Board in the UPSC after retirement as a member quite a few times when I happened to sit on the other side of the table, something that gave me great happiness and satisfaction. I also have been coaching aspirants in mock interviews in Rau's Study Circle since quite a few years.

After the interview, I waited for the result anxiously. One day I was told that the result would be declared in the evening. In those days the result used to be pasted outside the office building of the Press Information Bureau. Along with Jagdish Chandra, another Assistant in the Railway Board and my batchmate, I walked to Parliament Street to see the result. Chandra belonged to the Scheduled Caste (SC) category but wasn't sure of getting through even in the reserved quota for SC candidates. He was the only one apart from me to have appeared for this exam from the Railway Board that year. We scanned the list anxiously—and to our delight we were both on it! He got the

Indian Postal Service, but I was quite low in the list and was told by knowledgeable people later on that I might get the offer of the post of a Section Officer in some ministry, nothing more. For quite some time, there was no offer for me. July went by. All those who had got into the Indian Foreign Service (IFS), IAS, IPS and other Class I services got their letters of appointment and went to the National Academy of Administration, Mussoorie, for the foundational course. Obviously, I had missed the bus. I started preparing for the next attempt in the following year.

In the first week of December, as I was lying down in the afternoon on the charpoy in the veranda, my father came home. I was rather surprised to see him as he used to return from work late in the evening. I don't recall why I was home that day. But while walking in, he happily announced that I had made it to the IPS! I couldn't believe it and jumped up from the charpoy. 'Who told you?' I asked him. He said it was Balbir, my friend in the Railway Board. It so happened that Balbir was informed about this by someone he knew and he rang up my father in his office. That was why my father came home to break the news as we didn't have a telephone in those days. In fact, there was no telephone in the entire colony. It was a big luxury and getting a landline telephone connection would take years.

We all were overjoyed. My father was extremely happy because all his efforts had finally borne fruit. However, we waited for the formal letter to come before breaking the news to others. It finally came a few days later, giving us immense joy and relief. I got the call late due to reasons best known to God and the mandarins of the mighty bureaucracy in North Block, New Delhi.

However, in three and a half years, roughly from May 1964 to December 1967, I managed from being an LDC to the IPS by climbing the stairs of a UDC and Assistant in between. My record of clearing all the competitions in which I had appeared in the first attempt remained intact. But it was more due to the kindness of God and my sheer good luck. I wasn't that capable. Maybe it was because of good karmas in my previous births. Otherwise, how could I make it with such a poor academic record and not being exceptionally bright or knowledgeable?

Chapter 3

Joining the IPS and Training

I was straightaway asked to join at the National Police Academy at Mount Abu in Rajasthan as I had missed the foundational course at Mussoorie, and the IPS probationers had moved to the Police Academy for police training from there. But before that, a few formalities had to be completed and some preparation made. I underwent a medical examination at Safdarjung Hospital as mandated, a bond had to be signed, and since I was leaving home for the first time for a long period, I had to stock up on clothes as well.

I went to the New Delhi Railway Station to get my train ticket booked to Abu Road, unlike today when one can buy tickets online from the comfort of one's home. I had booked my ticket for 23 December 1967. The last thing I did was to go for a haircut two days before my departure. I was ready to leave with a trunk full of clothes and a holdall (a large rectangular bag with handles and carrying straps in which bedsheets, pillows, a quilt/blankets were packed), as was the norm those days while travelling by train, an item not seen these days. We had two holdalls at home for a long time and discarded them only some years ago.

On D-day, there were more than three dozen relatives, friends and well-wishers to give me a send-off in the evening at the New Delhi Railway Station's designated platform. I vividly recall that it was dusk and was drizzling at the time. I was overwhelmed by the affection showered on me. After some time, I boarded the train to travel towards my new destiny as a police officer—a most unlikely profession for me, a mild-mannered person. I had neither dreamt of joining this profession nor had anyone in the family joined the police till then.

Next evening, I got down at Abu Road from where I had to go Mount Abu, the only hill station of Rajasthan, at a distance of about 30 kilometres. Very few people had got down at the station. I noticed one plump young man and sensing that he could be a new batchmate, I walked over to him to greet him. He was Madhur Kumar Singh. A jovial fellow from Jaunpur in UP, he was full of life and a great companion. Like me, he too had got his appointment letter for the IPS late. We travelled together by taxi to the police academy. Later, I discovered that eight of us had got a late appointment. Incidentally, it was only in 1967 that the name of the institution for our training was changed from the Central Police Training College (CPTC) since its inception in 1948 to the National Police Academy.

I can't help but recount our first encounter with Inspector Tewari. On inquiries, we both were directed towards his office. He was in uniform. Once we told him that we were new probationers, he stood up, saluted us and said 'Jai Hind, Sir'. We also stood up. Respectfully, he asked us to sit down. I had never been addressed as 'Sir' before and felt both awkward yet happy about this newly acquired status. We realized that we had to get used to this new norm of being addressed.

He went through the papers and told us that we would be lodged in Palanpur House, where senior officers were generally accommodated, till a room was made ready for us in the main building called the Rajputana Hostel Estate (RHE). The other hostel at some distance was called Jodhpur House. He also told us that we should get ready for physical training (PT) in shorts the next morning when we would have to get up at 4 a.m. Of course, he said, we would be woken up by an orderly who would also serve us tea.

In winters, Mount Abu remains quite cold. The very thought of getting up early in the morning for PT made both of us dread it! But we had no option. Arrangements were made for us and a double bedroom allotted to us. We had hardly settled there when we were informed that a barber had come to cut our hair. Even though Madhur and I told the orderly that we'd had haircuts, the orderly insisted that we needed a new one from the 'police barber' in accordance with training norms. Having no choice, we obliged. The barber shaved off our hair above the ears, all around, and shortened the hair on top as much as he could. When I looked at myself in the mirror, I was horrified and unable to recognize myself!

More was yet to come. In the morning when we were woken up and tea was brought by the orderly, I went to the bathroom before having tea whereas Madhur had tea while sitting on the bed. He told me that this is what was meant by 'bed tea'! I was learning.

An Ustad (a trainer of the Havildar rank), who had come to lead us out to the parade ground, blew a whistle and our orderly asked us to move out of the room. We were made to join a group of probationers at some distance running towards the main parade ground. My God! What a cruelty! In that freezing winter to make us run in the early morning, when it was still dark, filled me with unhappiness and dislike for the place and the police academy. Both of us being heavyset, Madhur and I sat down on the road after some minutes, breathless, but the Ustad would have none of it. He asked us to get up and run.

Shortly afterwards, I heard the voice of a probationer running beside me, '*Hazoor, aap yahan kyon tashrif laye. Yeh sharifon ki jagah nahin hai* (Why have you come here? It is not a place for decent people)!'

'*Aap bhi to aye hain* (You have also come),' I replied.

'*Hazoor hamari to kismet phooti thi. Aap ki kismet ko kya hua tha* (I had bad luck, but why you?)' he said.

Later I came to know that he was Waris Hayat Khan (Daboo Mian) from Bihar. He was a batchmate full of life, sowing the first seed of hatred in my mind for the establishment. Anyway, I moved ahead with great difficulty. I suddenly noticed that someone had stepped on my right shoe deliberately from the back, forcing my foot to slip out of the PT shoe. I had to stop abruptly, causing a disruption of the entire squad and compelling the Ustad to shout at us. I looked back at the person who had done the mischief and he merely smiled. It was B.B. Mishra from Orissa (now Odisha) as I came to know later. It was a kind of ragging, a welcome to the newcomers. We have been very good friends since then.

At the parade ground called the Trevor Oval Polo Ground, I had the first *darshan* (sight) of T.B. Spadigam, the dark-complexioned, heavily built, tough guy from Goa who was the Chief Drill Instructor (CDI) with the rank of a DSP, and G.A. Burge, from New Zealand, who was the Assistant Director (AD) in charge of outdoor activities of the rank of a Superintendent of Police (SP). The CDI was a terror on the ground but shy like a bride off it. The new among us were allotted to different sections and I was sent to the F Section. Inspector Joseph was the in-charge of this section assisted by Havildar Vasdev normally addressed as the Ustad, a very pleasant but tough person. It was also for the first time that year that a few ex-army short service commissioned officers had been inducted into the IPS and other services.

While I was still in Palanpur House, S. Ramakrishnan (Ramu) and R.K. Handa, my IPS batchmates, came to meet me. It was a pleasant surprise as Ramu was a friend of my college classmate Natarajan. I had met him earlier once in Delhi along with Natarajan. Ramu later introduced me to rum and I took to it like a fish in water! After a few days, we were shifted to Rajputana Hostel. I was allotted a big room on the first floor near the Mess, and R.K. Sharma from Delhi, who had also joined late like me, was my roommate. There was no flush system in the toilet but we had separate thunder boxes (wooden commodes). I was mortally afraid when sitting on it as it creaked and made a kind of musical sound—a hilarious situation!

I used to avoid shaving on Tuesdays, the day dedicated to Lord Hanuman, lest the god got annoyed! But the CDI was definitely irritated when he closely inspected our section and saw me with stubby facial hair just like the other Hanuman disciples there. He asked us to fall out, double up to the Mess and rush back after shaving within 10 minutes, failing which we would be punished and made to run four rounds of the parade ground. Since that day, I have shaved regularly every day in the morning in deference to the orders of Spadigam at the risk of annoying Lord Hanuman. Believe me, I have not come to much grief due to the annoyance of the Lord. I continue to obey these orders during holidays and even now after retirement.

I went to the tailor, a Sikh, who stitched half of a dozen each of khaki shorts, shirts, bush shirts, trousers, and one set of breeches for riding in addition to close collared white and black dinner suits (*bandhgala*s). They were all on loan. Books were bought from Patel, the owner of the bookshop, and we also stocked up brown shoes, khaki socks, cap, normal belts and a cross belt, stars, baton and a sword. Gradually, I got to know all the probationers from all parts of India, opening my horizons further. B.B. Banerji, IP was the Director, A.K. Bannerjee was the Deputy Director and we had quite a few Assistant Directors and other staff teaching us various subjects like law, forensic science, map reading, wireless communication, intricacies of the engine of the jeep, among other skills. However, most of the teachers were boring.

Slowly, I got used to the grind. The busy schedule began with PT in the morning, followed by the parade, then baths and breakfast, followed by indoor classes and the evening sports period. Hockey was compulsory, so was riding. There was too much emphasis on physical work but it benefitted me in the sense that I lost about 20 kilograms of weight in three months and from a fat boy became a boy of normal weight.

I had my share of training, knocking the wooden horse, climbing the rope—unsuccessfully most of the time—push-ups on the beam, jumping and crossing hurdles, cross-country races, lathi and baton drills, saluting etiquettes and a plethora of other exercises. And enjoying the famous sarcastic nuggets of Spadigam to probationers like 'Don't hang there like a bat' when one couldn't lift up one's body while doing push-ups, 'Don't look a taxi driver' when a probationer was not wearing the peak cap correctly, and so on. Over a period of time, he became a darling of the batch, like for each of the batches before and after us.

Another formidable character was the riding instructor, Thakur Janak Singh. When someone would fall from a horse, he would say, 'Why have you dismounted without my permission?', among other gems. He was sarcastic like Spadigam many times. The indoor classes were mostly boring in which most of us used to feel sleepy, except KTPs (keen type probationers), or pass naughty notes and cartoons of teachers. The sports period in the afternoon was really enjoyable, unlike the riding period which most of us dreaded as invariably a few of us would fall from the horses during each session, and it would be a big topic of discussion in the evenings. I'm reminded of the annual Sports Day where there were only two participants in the event of the javelin throw. A third one was needed to have the first, second and third positions. The anchor, I think it was C.D. Sahay, was asking for volunteers for this event. I opted for it without knowing how to throw a javelin, but ensured I got the third position for myself.

I still remember our first day at the Shooting Range where we were taken to learn firing. When my group fired the first shot in the lying position at the targets, after practice with blank guns, Spadigam shouted, 'Who is at number 6?' I suddenly realized that I was the one at number 6 and got up, bracing myself for a firing from him for something wrong I'd done. He looked at me and said, 'Well done. You hit the bull in the very first shot.' I was shocked and surprised. It was a fluke because after that, my remaining shots were washed out, going far away from the target.

A great respite during the indoor classes was when we ran to the pigeon holes during the break to look for letters received from home. Gone are those days of writing and receiving letters, mostly inland. During our classes, I could never understand map reading and that ignorance remains till date—I'm sure that this must have brought down my seniority quite a few notches. But who cared! Of course, I topped in the Urdu language although it is a different matter that there were just two students learning Urdu. By the way, I did improve my final position considerably in the merit list at the end.

Going round the manmade Nakki Lake, a magical place for nature lovers, in the evening was refreshing and was like a compulsory activity for most of us. Years later when I visited Nakki Lake, I was disappointed to see its muddy water and the crowding and commercialization that had spoiled it. I also visited the world-famous Jain Dilwara temples with their splendid architecture in marble constructed between the 11th and 13th centuries.

I had made a lot of friends. I also noticed Punjabis were in a large number there, almost 30, perhaps, out of around 80 probationers. These days, the intake of Punjabis into the civil services has reduced considerably. Perhaps they are going towards greener pastures.

At the breakfast table in the Mess, I discovered my infinite ignorance about the different ways the humble egg could be cooked. To experience the sight of non-vegetarian food in the bowls of chicken curry was a challenge. Some smart people like G.N. Das would sit at the table next to the kitchen and grab chunks of meat whereas others would crib that they couldn't get enough. He would pile his plate with so much rice that he was often teased by the others who would ask, 'Please pass on the rice bowl,' pointing to his plate! Food wasn't good but tolerable. I had begun eating non-vegetarian food. There were weekly formal dinners when we had to wear *bandhgala*s.

Once in the Mess, after a taunt about long hair by Spadigam, Uday Rajwade and few others shaved off their hair, invited him for dinner and sat beside him on the high table for dinner! Next day he noticed one of them marching slowly and thundered, 'You Buddhist, this is a parade ground, not your bloody dining table!' By then we were all used to his ways and didn't mind his remarks. In fact, it was always fun to recount his nuggets as I'm doing even now, writing this book after about 54 years of training in Mount Abu. He was a strong disciplinarian and taught us a lot.

One highlight was the visit of Punjab Assembly Speaker Joginder Singh Mann whose son Simranjit Singh Mann was our batchmate. Asha Parekh, the well-known actor, also visited Mount Abu in those days. Occasionally, we would have cultural programmes and many probationers would participate enthusiastically. For example, Sangliana, a Mizo from Manipur, used to play the guitar. The New Year celebration on 31 December 1967 was enjoyable as were parties at Chacha Museum, a shop owned by a Sikh gentleman, which was next to the parade ground. Many probationers enjoyed life to the fullest in their own different ways. Later, some of them got selected for the IAS and left the Academy. I had also appeared in the examination again in the next year but could only clear the exam for the Central services, which I was not interested in. Cadre allotment was always big news and I was happy to be given the UT cadre since I came from Delhi.

I must recount an episode which I cannot forget. When

Ramakrishnan and I were travelling to Delhi by train during the Holi holidays in March 1968, I forgot or lost my suitcase while boarding the train at the Abu Road Railway Station. Noticing it missing, we got down from our compartment and started looking for it on the platform. In the meanwhile, the train started moving. We were too far away from our compartment and even when as we ran, we knew that we wouldn't be able to reach our compartment as the train's speed had become fast. We could not get into any near compartment as the entry doors were closed. Being young and fit, we hung on the window bars of the first compartment we could reach, a very foolish thing to do as we could have lost our lives that day. But it didn't matter then.

Imagine clinging to the thin iron bars of a train window with feet hanging in the air outside a fast-moving train, very much like a film scene! We could have been struck by a pole or something else and been killed. People inside that compartment who noticed us must have thought that we were criminals, so they did not open the door of that first-class compartment in spite of our banging the door and pleading to them to open it. Finally, they relented. Even today when we think of that episode we shiver in fright. But when one is young, one does idiotic things, isn't it?

It was time for our Bharat Darshan to acquire a first-hand perspective of the 'real' India. In fact, it was a Zone Darshan for us as four groups were covering different states. My group, led by our instructor Gurcharan Singh, visited Kharagpur in West Bengal, Bhubaneshwar, Cuttack and Paradip in Odisha, and Madhya Pradesh's Bhopal and Mandu, among other places. At Puri in Odisha, I recall seeing the sea for the first time in my life and was overawed by its vastness. The SP there had treated us to a grand dinner.

Once we were back, the final examination was due. Indoor and outdoor exams in riding, PT and other disciplines were also held. Then preparations for the Passing-Out Parade (POP) started. Y.B. Chavan, the then Union Home Minister, took the salute at the POP. Sunder Singh, an ex-army officer, was declared the best cadet and B.N. Mishra won the Tonk Cup in riding. Finally, it was time to say goodbye to the Academy and to lovely Mount Abu.

We left for Ahmedabad for our army attachment. We were invited for drinks by Major General Hazare in a Mess. Since I was new to drinks, I went to the bar and wanting to taste scotch whisky, asked the bartender, 'Please give me scotch.'

'Which scotch, Sir?' he asked. I was surprised at his ignorance and asked, 'Haven't you heard of scotch?'

'Sorry, Sir, I'll just pour scotch for you,' he said and did the needful. He must have smiled at my ignorance as I hadn't heard of the various brands of scotch whisky. I drank quite a few pegs rather fast and then passed out on a bench oblivious to the surroundings. After a while, I was literally lifted and taken back to where we were staying. I vomited copiously that day.

While experiencing life in the army, we were sent to Dharangadhara in the Rann of Kutch. Ramakrishnan was in that group too. It was a desert and we were attached to an artillery unit which had pitched tents somewhere in the desert to carry out trials of new field guns that had just been acquired. The very first evening, we were enjoying coke with rum when I noticed that Ramu had taken too much of it and wasn't steady on his feet, so we asked him to go to his tent. He returned as he could not find it, so we went together to his tent. Later, we were taken to the field where we saw the exercise of firing of big guns. It was a great first-hand experience.

After the attachment, we had to go the states allotted to us where our state training had to start. I came to Delhi and was asked to report at the Punjab Police Training College at Phillaur for state training. This PTC, located within a fort near Ludhiana, which is about 18 kilometres from Phillaur, had a formidable reputation especially for tough physical training, and was called a 'Qila' as it was housed in an old fort. In those days, officers of the UT, Punjab and Haryana cadres were trained there. With me in the UT cadre were S. Ramakrishnan, D.K. Kashyap, G.S. Pandher, Arun Morarka, A.K. Puri, R.K. Sharma, Puran Singh and D.S. Amist (both DSPs). I was allotted one room to share with Puri and Puran. (Puran passed away in May 2022.) It was December 1968 and very cold in Punjab. And indeed, PT there was a little tougher than Mount Abu. We were made to run ahead with full heavy attire in front of the lower ranks being trained there for promotional courses. We were trained to perform the duty of a sentry at the quarter guard and sleep there in a tent with a rifle attached to us all the time for one week. It was tough PT, almost like physical torture.

In the Mess, dinner was always served at 8 p.m. sharp when we all had to be present in the formal uniform. It was a kind of drill. We were financially very tight and once we had no money to eat in the Mess. G.S. Pandher, our Mess Secretary, announced that we would get three *chapatti*s each with *dal* that evening as the last supper and after that, the kitchen would be closed as there was no money at all! Our salary was around Rs 520, which was not enough for the Mess and other expenses, and we all were shy of asking our family members to send money. Some of us had already done that while at Mount Abu and didn't have the heart to ask for it again. Our principal, J.R. Chhabra, the IG with a reputation for toughness, bailed us out by loaning us money from the Welfare Fund. Once in a while, some of us would go to Ludhiana to see films.

From Phillaur we were called to Delhi in January 1969 to see the Republic Day arrangements of the Delhi Police. I was attached with Markandey Singh, SP (Crime), who was supervising arrangements very close to the India Gate. He later became the Lieutenant Governor of Delhi when Chandra Shekhar was the Prime Minister as both were close friends from earlier days. On our return to Phillaur, examinations were held about a month later. Only four of us passed in the final examination and I happened to be one of them.

Back to the Delhi Police by March 1969, we started our field training in various branches of police functioning. We had to write a diary of our daily work and training to be shown every week to the DIG (Range), R.D. Singh, who used to ask tough questions. We had to read the Punjab Police Manual thoroughly as it was applicable to the Delhi Police. He took our training seriously unlike some of us trainees. To help us with transportation, the Delhi Police Headquarters got Vespa scooters allotted to us on a priority basis and a loan of about Rs 3,000 per head was also given to us for purchasing the same. All of our scooters were steel grey in colour. I stayed at home since I belonged to Delhi while those who came from places other than Delhi were accommodated in the Mess in the Police Lines in Kingsway Camp. I was allotted to the South District for training. H.C. Jatav was the SP of the district. The Delhi Police had three districts in those days with one Deputy Commissioner (DC) for the entire area of Delhi and an Additional District Magistrate (ADM) for each district. Today there are more than a dozen districts. There was no Police Commissioner system then in Delhi.

My first police station training was in the Mandir Marg police station and Pandit Jugraj Chand, the Station House Officer (SHO), was sincere in teaching me. Once he asked me to come to the police station at about 11.30 p.m. so that we could do night patrolling. I reached on time and was thinking that we would go in a jeep, but to my surprise, he and some of his juniors started walking on foot. I asked him about the jeep to which he replied, 'Sir, we should see our jurisdiction on foot so that we are thoroughly familiar with our area and what happens there. Please join us and let's walk.'

I liked his remark but the prospect seemed daunting as he told me that we would walk till dawn broke and go over as much of the area as possible. We walked towards Panchkuian Road on the left side and after some time, I noticed many men and more women briskly walking barefooted towards the Gol Dakhana (circular post office), short of Parliament Street. I thought that something serious had happened as these people were almost running, but he told me that they were all going towards Bangla Sahib Gurudwara for prayers.

After some time, I was told that in his jurisdiction, there were some incidents of purse snatching in buses by criminals who were brandishing knives and robbing people of wallets and cash or whatever they could lay their hands on. In the weekly crime meeting, he was pulled up by the SP for being unable to catch the criminals involved and stop this crime.

About two days later when I reached the police station in the morning, Jugraj Chand told me that he had apprehended the two criminals who were committing crimes in his area with the long, sharp knives in their possession and that they were in the lock-up at last. He took me there to see them. I congratulated him and asked him how he had succeeded. Then he confided in me, admitting that he had actually caught two innocent beggars from his area, showing them as criminals to satisfy the SP. As for the knives, he had procured two Rampuri *chakus* (named after the town of Rampur, UP, these knives are famous for their long and sharp blades) from Paharganj. His action eased some pressure on him from the SP though such incidents continued. While telling me the truth, he told me that I needed to know about such tricks used by the lower staff so that I would be better at supervision when I became the chief of a district. He also told me to keep this information to myself for his sake. Thanks to him for sharing this. He took a big risk in telling me the truth but I was grateful that he had tried to teach me by letting me into the secret.

With my first salary in Delhi, I bought a watch for my father, a first for him, from Chandni Chowk for Rs 80.

My SP, H.C. Jatav, took great interest in my training. A thorough police professional, he was earlier an officer in the Punjab cadre. He used to take me along when a law and order situation had to be handled, during his supervision of investigations as well as his inspection of police stations, which was a useful learning experience for me. Sometimes, he would even bring lunch for me from home. He used to make me sit next to him in his office chamber while doing his work or interacting with the police and non-police visitors. Tough while training, he would give me no respite. I felt its bitter taste when I decided to complete my MA from Delhi University.

As I had mentioned earlier, I could not complete my MA when in the Railway Board as my father had fallen sick. I had forgotten about it since I was preparing for the civil services, but I discovered that there was a last chance for those who wanted to appear for the MA exam in the old course that year as the syllabus had since changed. I decided to take a shot at it. That is when I asked for leave, and was flatly refused by Jatav. He reluctantly agreed to give me casual leaves on those days when I had to appear for the examinations. I was disappointed but still took the chance.

My training continued in some other branches also. During the training period, I fell from a horse I was riding in the ground near the Old Police Lines in the Civil Lines area. The fault was entirely mine as I mounted the horse without wearing breeches. When the horse reared its front legs high up in the air, I couldn't handle it and fell face down. I started bleeding profusely from the face and was injured on some other parts of the body also. I was rushed to the nearest police hospital in the Old Police Lines. The doctor noticed a severe cut above my upper lip that needed stitching, which he did there and then. My face was badly bruised. It took me time to recover but I couldn't shave off my moustache due to the stitches above the upper lip, so perforce, I grew a moustache. That scar still remains on my upper lip.

Meanwhile, I was deputed to go the Lal Bahadur Shastri National Academy of Administration for the foundational course along with others who had joined directly at Mount Abu and had missed this course. I had an interesting first day at the Academy. I had reached in the afternoon and was allotted a room, which I had to share with another probationer already there, K.S. Swaminathan, an IAS probationer who was allotted the Madhya Pradesh cadre. He was not in the room at that time. I unpacked my clothes with the help of the orderly and hung one of my coats on the wall. I went out and when I returned after some time, I found that my coat was missing. I could only guess that my roommate had come to the room in my absence, had worn my coat and gone out again—or it could be a theft. I was worried. After I waited a bit, he walked in wearing my coat and said smilingly, 'It's a smart coat. Fitted me well!' It was a great introduction. He was an ex-army officer, who was in the 1969 batch, doing the foundational course. We hit it off and he was great company. As a pair, we also won the three-legged race in a sports event in the Academy some time later.

While at the Mussoorie Academy, I was reading the *Hindustan Times* one day when I spotted a small notice mentioning my name. To my pleasant surprise, I read that Bhushan Lal Vohra had passed the MA Economics (old course) examination of the Delhi University. I had topped the university also in this course as I was the only one who had cleared it out of the few who had appeared for the exam. However, it was not even a second division and I kept my record of not scoring more than 50 per cent in any academic examination! Considering that for three years I had not studied my subject and got no time for preparation either, I think it was no mean achievement. I patted myself on the back.

Madhur Kumar Singh, my batchmate and friend, was a well-read and well-informed person, with a great sense of humour. He couldn't live without a drink in the evening, finding a new excuse to have alcohol every day. First, it was that he was not getting engaged, so he needed a drink to drown his sorrow. When he did get engaged, he started celebrating the event every evening with a drink. He had asked his fiancée to write him a letter every day, then he would drink when the letter came to say 'Cheers!' to his happiness, but he would also drink when the letter didn't come to overcome his grief!

I enjoyed my stay in Mussoorie. Strolling in the pleasant weather on the Mall Road with tourists thronging there, attractive shops, restaurants like Whispering Windows and visits to scenic places like the Kempty Falls, with its cascades of water, were enjoyable. Today, Mussoorie is no longer the same, its old-world charm whittled away by commercialization and crowds of tourists. At that time, all probationers would get suits tailored on loan at a shop called Jacksons (real name Jai Kishan). Now this shop sells only readymade garments. Even the buildings in the Academy were architecturally in the colonial style, but now we have modern swanky buildings there except for a symbolic old double-storey structure that houses the office of the Director, which I saw during the Golden Jubilee Reunion of our batch in the Academy about four years ago. The barrack-type structures with sloping green-tiled roofs and rooms below had been demolished. It used to be a hotel owned by a Britisher before the Academy came up there.

After completing training at the Academy, I returned to Delhi to rejoin the training schedule. I was posted to the Hauz Khas police station for training where Kulbhushan Kumar was the SHO. I saw how he and his staff used to avoid registering First Information Reports (FIRs) or downgrade offences while registering them. I was also sent on a raid of an opium smuggler's house along with a very competent Assistant Sub-Inspector (ASI) who had taken along some opium himself so that he could show he had recovered it from the accused. He did this as he was sure that the accused would throw the opium out of the window, which is what actually happened. When I told him the opium thrown out could be shown as evidence, he said that the smuggler would deny it and would not be convicted because we didn't get it from his possession. He had composed a perfect FIR in advance in this case and had shown it to me so that I could see how it should be written.

One day, a couple came to the police station complaining that their maid had stolen their cash and jewellery. When she was traced and caught, she confessed that she had indeed stolen the money and jewellery but that she was in dire need of money. She returned everything, but the SHO was keen to arrest her as the case had been worked out even though by then the FIR had not been registered. I intervened and asked the SHO to let her go, pointing out that she had a small child and if she had confessed, returned the stolen material and apologized, why send her to jail? I said that her life and that of the child would be spoiled. He agreed with me and the maid was released.

Kulbhushan Kumar asked me to buy a plot in Hauz Khas measuring about 500 square yards which cost around Rs 20,000 at that time. He knew about it as it was near the police station. I neither had the money nor the inclination to buy it. I was also of the view that one shouldn't buy property in the area where one is working, my thinking reflecting the idealism of a young man. He told me that I would repent it one day. Now I am living in a two-room DDA flat in Saket not far from Hauz Khas, not in a fancy house which I could have built on that plot.

I learnt during training that the police force considered itself as the ruler, that it was corrupt and arrogant, indulged in malpractices and illegalities, but also had faced difficulties in its functioning with long hours of work, no holidays, stress, poor living conditions for the lower ranks, inadequate salaries, and many other drawbacks. But it is also a very noble profession. I realized it most during my posting as the Additional SP of Central District later on. It was when we were successful in recovering a kidnapped child and restoring him to the grateful parents who came and tried to touch my feet, giving me and the police blessings. The police do give instant relief and justice in many cases, which the people want. I didn't see any political interference as the Delhi Police was not working under the Chief Minister of Delhi, the police was directly under the Ministry of Home Affairs and worked with the Lieutenant Governor of Delhi.

While my training was going on, India was passing through major political events. President Zakir Hussain died on 3 May 1969 while still in office. The Election Commission announced that the election of his successor would be on 16 August 1969. Indira Gandhi was against the nomination of Congress leader Neelam Sanjiva Reddy for this post but he was favoured by senior Congress Party leaders called the Syndicate. She supported V.V. Giri as an independent candidate against Reddy and appealed to party legislators to 'vote according to their conscience'. Many backed her and Giri won. On 12 November, she was expelled from her own party by its president Nijalingappa on charges of 'fostering a cult of personality' and violating party discipline. She retaliated by setting up a rival party which was called the Congress (R). As many as 446 members out of 705 of the All-India Congress Committee walked over to her side. K. Kamraj and Morarji Desai were the leaders of the Congress (O) and this group led state governments in Bihar, Gujarat and Karnataka. The split was also seen as a Left-wing/Right-wing division. Whereas Indira wanted to use a populist agenda in order to mobilize support for the party, the Syndicate wanted a Right-wing agenda. Later, Indira Gandhi's group became the real Congress and the Congress (O) merged with the Janata Party.

My training got over in December, 1969. One of the highlights of my training period was commanding a company in a parade in Old Police Lines, Kingsway Camp, Delhi, in which Prime Minister Indira

Gandhi took the salute. My colleagues also commanded companies. That black and white photograph (colour photography had not yet started) with her after the parade still adorns my study along with some other memorable photographs of times gone by.

When the training period was over, all of us in the batch got postings. I was posted as the ASP (Headquarters), North District, Delhi.

Chapter 4

Posting in Delhi

My office was on the second floor of Tis Hazari Courts in north Delhi in a very large room. Nikhil Kumar of the 1963 batch was my SP. He was a very capable, tough officer and I learnt a lot from him. I would like to recount few events of that period.

All the Sub-Divisional Police Officers (SDPOs) in the district were allotted a jeep, but I did not get one. Since I was equal in rank and status to them, I asked the SP to give me a jeep. He told me to find out if any jeep could be spared in the district, and if so, he would give that to me. However, when I worked out the availability and the requirement of various officers and police stations, I realized that all the jeeps were being used. I learnt my lesson and didn't raise this topic again with him. He then told me that whenever I went to him or any senior with a problem, I should also suggest a solution. Another lesson for me was that I needed to check and recheck the text of whatever I wrote or signed. I learnt this when a copy of a press note on something went to him. He called me and told me that many addressees in the list were no longer there—it was an obsolete list and I should have checked it.

In the office, my greatest challenge was accountant Gita Ram. He always expected me to sign the papers put up by him. If I questioned him or asked him to do something, he would quote the rules. He wouldn't bother to change his stance even if I got angry. Being fed up, one day I went to the SP and complained about him. Nikhil Kumar told me that it was for me to tackle him. I should use my powers and take action against him and for that, I would get full support. Emboldened, I went back and studied the extent of my powers and discovered that I could even suspend Gita Ram. That was my turning point. I also started studying the financial rules seriously, though I never liked them. A week later, I was ready to confront him. I told him to do something, and as usual, he flatly refused. I wrote my orders on the file and told him that if he did not do it, I would suspend him. He was taken aback. He didn't expect such a reaction, more so because nobody had ever told him that as per the rules, non-compliance with an order could lead to suspension. When he said that I could not do it, I firmly told him that I could. He gave in because finally he realized that I was right. After that he became very subservient and I had no problems with him. In fact, my functioning improved as he started cooperating with me, even teaching me. Again, it was a lesson learnt—know the rules thoroughly.

Since I became entitled to have a residential telephone, it was installed at my home in Bharat Nagar—the first in the colony which came as a big boon for all the residents. This kept us quite busy, calling people when their phone calls came or welcoming them when they wanted to use the phone, making a hole in my pocket as I had to pay for all the private calls. But we didn't mind. Fortunately, I had an orderly by then and he helped in conveying messages and calling people from their homes.

To give me an opportunity to learn some fieldwork, Nikhil Kumar also gave me the additional charge of SDPO, Kingsway Camp, when

Balwant Singh, the SDPO, went on leave for some time. When I took the charge the next day, a murder was committed in the evening at the Kingsway Camp chowk. I had just sat down to have dinner at home in Bharat Nagar when I got a call from the SHO, Kingsway Camp police station, informing me about this murder. I left my food and rushed to the spot, where the SHO showed me the dead body lying on a cot with multiple knife wounds. The body was turned upside down to show me the stabs at the back also. It was a brutal killing. Unable to stand the sight, I felt very sick. The SHO told me that steps were being taken to nab the culprit. Returning home, I couldn't even sleep properly after seeing the gruesome injuries on the corpse.

Next morning, when I met the SP and gave him details about the murder and efforts to catch the accused, I also told him how I had rushed to the spot, leaving my dinner uneaten. I wanted to show how prompt my response had been, but he told me, 'Bhushi, never leave your food like that because in police work if you leave it, you may have to stay hungry for a long time if the case requires your presence. Besides, by your rushing to the spot, did the murdered fellow get up and was the accused arrested by you? There is the entire police station staff to investigate. Your role is supervisory and for that there is no urgency.' This was yet another lesson for me.

Once there was a dispute between two warring groups of Sikhs led by Jathedar Santokh Singh and Richhpal Singh, respectively, over the control of Gurudwara Sisganj in Chandni Chowk. The main gate of the gurudwara was locked. I was asked by the SP to stay in police station Kotwali adjoining the gurudwara round the clock for about a fortnight to ensure that there was no forcible entry or law and order situation. The dispute got sorted out later when the main gate itself was removed by us and the two leaders were sent to the Patiala and Agra jails separately.

I can never forget the sight of the basement of the gurudwara where currency coins offered during worship were weighed to calculate the total sum rather than counted because the amount was too large!

Supervising the arrangements during the Ram Lila, the drama based on the Ramayana, the great epic, celebrations was enjoyable. Eating popular delicacies like *daribe ki jalebi*, *dahi bhalla* from a *matke wala* (who used earthenware pots) near Punjab National Bank, *parantha*s from Paranthe Wali Gali or sweets from Chaina Ram or Ghantewala confectioners, all from the bustling bazars of Old Delhi, was a great joy. I used to invite Veena and Anita, my sister's daughters from Subhash Nagar, to watch these processions and other celebrations. I was also a part of the police arrangements during Independence Day celebrations at Red Fort on 15 August that year. Prime Minister Indira Gandhi had unfurled the national flag and delivered a speech from the ramparts of the Red Fort. When I was a student, I had come to Red Fort with my father to see the celebrations and listen to the speech of the Prime Minister. All this was a great learning experience.

Another duty which I had to do once in a while was night patrolling as I was the night gazetted officer by rotation for the entire area of Delhi and sometimes for North District also. I learnt driving a jeep at night, taking advantage of the deserted roads. On one of my rounds, I went to the Delhi Cantonment police station at night for checking and saw a sentry peacefully sleeping even though he was on duty. I picked up his rifle and came away. Alarm bells rang in the police station and the SHO then got in touch with me, pleading with me to return the rifle as he would lose his job. I relented. Once, while patrolling in Lajpat Nagar, I saw someone running away after seeing my police jeep. I got down and ran after him. Being young and fit, I was able to catch him after a short chase. On questioning him, he admitted that he was a thief and looking for a target when he saw the jeep. He was then handed over to the police station.

The SHOs in the district were efficient professionals and very effective in their area. All of them were very hard-working. Their supervisory officers, the SDPOs, were also good—Pandit Lal Chand, the DSP of the Kotwali sub-division, who had risen from the rank of a constable, was the most experienced one.

I was also appointed as a Security Officer with two visiting Heads of State, King Mahendra of Nepal and Sir Edward Heath, the British Prime Minister. In those days, the visiting Heads of State used to stay in the Rashtrapati Bhawan, the palatial official residence of the President of India. During my posting with the British Prime Minister, on the second or third day of his visit, I went to Rashtrapati Bhawan just before the beginning of his engagements. As I entered the lift to go to the first floor where he was staying, Indira Gandhi, the Prime Minister, rushed into the lift. I was shocked and overawed. I wished her 'Good morning' and she replied pleasantly and asked me whether I was the Security Officer to the British Prime Minister. I nodded. It was a rare moment seeing her so closely. She was stunningly beautiful. By then the lift stopped at the first floor and she stepped out. She had come to meet Sir Edward Heath. Yet another surprise was in store for me that morning. After I entered the drawing room of the visiting dignitary's suite, I started looking at some photographs and paintings on the wall with my back towards the bedroom of the Prime Minister. Suddenly, I felt a tap on my shoulder. As I looked back, it was Sir Edward Heath himself saying, 'Good morning, Security Officer!' I was taken aback. It was a fine gesture. He surprised me further when he graciously presented me with his autographed photograph at the time of his departure.

During this period, my parents decided that I should get married. So, the search started and some proposals discussed. During this period, unknown to me, the eldest brother of Sudesh, my friend from the colony, recommended that my matrimonial alliance should be with the daughter of his wife's sister. The name of the girl was Chander

Mohini. She was studying in the final year of BA in Miranda House, Delhi University. Her father R.P. Khanna, one of the directors of the Jaipur Golden Transport Company, had seen me during a pre-arranged visit to Jagdish Kapur at Bharat Nagar when I was called there on some pretext. I was then asked to meet Chander. I flatly refused on the ground that she was still a student. Jagdish Kapur then played smart. He forced his younger brother Sudesh to take me to Chander's house in Roop Nagar to meet her and then leave the decision to me. I was reluctant to go, but Sudesh insisted, saying that we should complete the formality of a visit as his elder brother had commanded it and I could say 'No' after it. As a friend, I gave in. Sudesh had a plaster on his right arm due to a fall some days earlier.

Against my wishes, Sudesh and I went to Roop Nagar, not very far from our colony, one morning in the first week of December 1969 on my Vespa scooter. Chander's family lived in a big house with a lawn and had all the modern-day amenities. I met Chander as she was ready to go to college. I had a brief chat with her over a cup of tea in the presence of her parents and found her to be a sweet girl. Back home I told my parents of my impression and the die was cast. Our engagement took place on her birthday that month on 27 February.

I have never forgiven Sudesh for being treacherous and almost forcing me to meet Chander! Whenever I met him later, I told him that I felt like strangulating him! Sudesh was my friend for a very long time, but unfortunately, we lost him to Covid in 2021. He was my benefactor on two main counts in life—one was that I was inspired to aim for the IPS by his other brother V.P. Kapur in 1961 when I saw what it meant to be a police officer and then my marriage, through which we became relatives.

After a few months of courtship, I got married on 7 May 1970 after Chander had appeared for her final examination leading to her graduation. Many of our relatives stayed with us for many days before and after the wedding. Since I had invited many senior officers, including the IG, L.S. Bisht, head of the Delhi Police, and my batchmates, I was very keen to reach the place of the assembly of the *baraat* on time. The venue was the Roshanara Road police station, which was close to the bride's place. Leaving behind almost the entire marriage party, I reached the place a little before time to be present when the IG arrived. To my disappointment, he did not come. In that colony of Roop Nagar there were quite a few weddings that evening. So, some of the officers, including Jatav, the SP who had trained me, attended some other function and after dinner when they went to congratulate the bridegroom, they found someone else. Ultimately, they located me at the right venue. The wedding photographs were in black and white then as colour photography had not made an advent nor was there any videography then.

We went to Nainital, the hill station in what is now the state of Uttarakhand, for our honeymoon for a week. It was my first flight. We took a Dakota aircraft for Pant Nagar, well known for its agricultural university close to Nainital. Chander, whom we had named Jyoti after the wedding, changing of the bride's name after marriage being a custom, had travelled by air earlier to Nepal as a student since her family was affluent. She still recalls that their group met Dev Anand and Zahida, the famous actors, while on a visit to Sikkim during the shooting of a film as their student tour was to Nepal, Darjeeling and Sikkim. In Nainital, I had booked a room in Alka Hotel, right on the side of the lake. That hotel is still there. We had a gala time boating in the Nainital Lake, enjoying panoramic views from the mountains, riding and, of course, eating in different restaurants.

After our return, a few days later my father took me aside one morning and advised me to shift to a government flat. His reason was that our house would be uncomfortable for Jyoti as she was used to the up-to-date facilities in her parental house. Moreover, he was far-sighted enough to want her to start looking after a home on her own from the beginning so that she would learn how to manage a household quickly. I protested as I wanted to continue staying with my parents, so he left the decision to me. Summer was at its peak and our house with its asbestos sheets was really hot, but he couldn't do much to reduce Jyoti's discomfort. We had electricity and a ceiling fan by then, but it didn't help much. All he could do to make her comfortable was to fix a small washbasin outside the bathroom. The greatest problem was that there was no flush system, which meant that the toilet was always smelly as the excreta were only picked up each morning. He also asked me to get cooking gas at home immediately though my mother did most of the cooking.

I felt that her parents had done great injustice to her by marrying her off to me but destiny has its own role to play. Perhaps her father had thought that she would be very comfortable in future and so decided to sacrifice her present. And my decision to stay on there in spite of my father's advice added to her misery. I must admit that she put up with it bravely. Because of this marriage, I was lucky to get a new family—we had many outings, gossip sessions, eating together in restaurants, visiting Mussoorie, seeing films with Jyoti's siblings, her younger brother Satish and two sisters Neelam and Geeta. For me, it was a welcome change from being alone earlier to have plenty of company now. A few months later, Jyoti was pregnant and we started looking forward to the new arrival but that was still some months away. During this period, her BA examination result was declared and she passed with good marks.

Meanwhile, life was going on. In January 1971, the UT of Himachal Pradesh was given statehood and the UT cadre was bifurcated. I remained in the UT cadre. Then on 31 March of that year, we welcomed the arrival of my daughter Archana in St Stephen's Hospital, Tis Hazari. I still recall that when I picked her up a few hours after her birth that morning and surveyed her body from head to toe, I marvelled at God's creation. What a miracle! The family was full of joy and we celebrated for days. For Jyoti, motherhood was a great blessing. For the comfort of the little baby, I hired a cooler for Rs 30 per month.

During this period, unfortunately, two of my batchmates Arun Morarka and D.K. Kashyap died in road accidents, bringing gloom to all of us. They were good friends and shaping well as officers.

Another drama was unfolding in Pakistan, which would have serious repercussions for it and India. In the general elections held there on 7 December 1970, the East Pakistan-based Awami League led by Sheikh Mujibur Rahman won an absolute majority by winning 160 seats in East Pakistan, while the Pakistan People's Party in West Pakistan won only 81 seats. But Mujibur Rahman was not made the Prime Minister as Zulfikar Ali Bhutto of West Pakistan, supported by President Yahya Khan, refused to hand over power to him. This led to huge unrest in East Pakistan, leading to the arrest of Mujibur Rahman. The Pakistani army went in for a severe crackdown, which resulted in genocide, rapes and many other brutalities. This led to the influx of about 10 million refugees into the neighbouring states of India from East Pakistan. There was a revolt there and an indigenous fighting force called the Mukti Bahini was raised and trained by India with a view to fight and win independence for East Pakistan as a separate country, Bangladesh.

The Pakistan Air Force launched pre-emptive air strikes on Indian air bases in the western sector, leading to a full-fledged war between the two countries. The Indian Army marched into West Pakistan backed by successful operations by the air force and the navy between 3 and 16 December 1971, the shortest war, with a decisive victory over Pakistan by capturing its territories. I recall the blackouts at night in those days for some protection from the expected bombs by the Pakistani Air Force. India responded as a nation on all fronts. The war ended with the surrender of Lieutenant General A.A.K. Niazi of the Pakistan Army in Dacca (now Dhaka) along with 93,000 Pakistani army ranks to Lieutenant General J.S. Aurora, the Eastern Command Army Commander, on 16 December 1971. India won the war in spite of huge support to Pakistan from the USA, which sent an aircraft carrier into the Bay of Bengal, but India also had the support of the USSR with which it had signed a Treaty of Peace and Friendship a short while ago.

East Pakistan became Bangladesh, an independent country. The religion-based theory on which Pakistan was created into East Pakistan and West Pakistan for Muslims was overturned with Bangladesh becoming independent on language basis, being Bengali-speaking.

Mujibur Rahman was released from the Pakistani jail and came to Delhi on the way to Dacca on 10 January 1972. I recall being on duty at the Palam airport that morning in South District. Even though I was the Additional SP of another district, M.B. Kaushal, SP, South District, had asked for me to assist him in police arrangements at the airport. I had a glimpse of the proud President of a new country that day. India's stock went high in the world and Indira Gandhi was also lauded in India and abroad. Earlier, she had won the general elections held in March that year with a handsome majority because of her populist agenda, including nationalising 14 major banks and later, by the abolition of privy purses of the erstwhile princes, etc.

However, most of the gains in the war with Pakistan were nullified, except for the creation of Bangladesh, in the Shimla Agreement in 1972 India signed with West Pakistan. With 93,000 Pakistani prisoners of war with us, Bhutto would have signed any agreement and the Kashmir problem could have been solved on our terms but alas, that wasn't the case. India should have got rid of the aggressors in the entire J&K region as then there would have been no Pakistan-Occupied Kashmir (POK). Like the unilateral ceasefire by Nehru earlier in 1948, after India had thrown out Pakistani aggressors but only halfway, this was a mistake committed by his daughter that let Pakistan off the hook. We could have got the entire POK back as that is our territory.

Sometime before the arrival of Mujibur Rahman in Delhi on his way to Dacca, our batch was due for the senior-scale promotions. All my batchmates senior to me in the merit list in Delhi got promoted but to my dismay, I was ignored. On some cadre posts meant for IPS officers, as laid down by the rules, non-cadre officers not belonging to the IPS, including a few who were promoted from the post of DSP, were promoted. I got very angry and wrote a representation directly to A.N. Jha, the then Lieutenant Governor of Delhi, quoting cadre rules and saying that by posting non-cadre officers to cadre posts, an injustice had been done to me by not promoting me. He forwarded the representation to Chief Secretary T.N. Chaturvedi who knew me a little as he was posted in the Mussoorie Academy when I was there for my foundational course. Apparently, the Lieutenant Governor had asked the Chief Secretary to do the course correction.

T.N. Chaturvedi called me to his office and smilingly said that I had created problems for the police department and asked me why I hadn't told him of this problem first rather than writing to the Lieutenant Governor. I apologized but he knew that being young, I was inexperienced, full of idealism and anger, so I had taken this step rather than first going to him. My action angered the IG and officers in the police headquarters, but they had to issue transfer orders of officers, posting cadre officers to cadre posts. While doing the needful, they, however, ensured that I was not promoted to teach me a lesson. I was crestfallen and for the first time, I got the feeling that even in the highest services, injustice is prevalent.

In the said transfers and postings, my Additional SP, North District, Prakash Singh, got posted out and Kulbir Singh of the 1965 batch was posted in his place. One day, while sitting with him, I lamented about the fact that I had not been promoted. When he asked me what could be done to rectify the situation, I replied that if one officer of the SP rank went on leave for a minimum period of two months, I could be promoted in accordance with the rules. He promptly said, 'I'll go on leave for two months.' I could not dissuade him and on the same day, he applied for leave. I was overwhelmed by his gesture and it was because of him that I finally got my promotion and posting in his place as the Additional SP in the North District itself in February in 1972. I have remained grateful to him forever. We became good friends since then and remained so till his sad demise some time ago.

During my posting as the Additional SP in the North District, H.K.L. Bhagat, a very junior Congress leader from East Delhi, once came to meet me. As he was sitting outside my office on a bench waiting to be called in, I saw him when I left for lunch at home but did not recognize him. When I returned after more than an hour, he was still sitting there. I asked my orderly who he was and he told me that he was a small-time politician who had come to meet me. He was asked to wait but since I suddenly left for lunch, the orderly had told him, '*Sahib ilaqe mein gaye hein, aap intenzaar kariye* (Sir has gone to the field. Please wait for him to come back to see him).' This was the standard sentence orderlies used when speaking to visitors if they didn't want to tell them about the whereabouts of the bosses. I called Bhagat in, gave him a cup of tea and helped him with a small problem that I could resolve.

Years later, Bhagat became a powerful minister (holding the Information and Broadcasting portfolio) in the cabinet of PM Rajiv Gandhi and helped in expanding the telecom infrastructure in a big way during the 1980s. TV had exploded in India. I happened to be DIG (Range), New Delhi, CRPF in 1985 and there was a CRPF guard at his bungalow. We were badly in need of a lot of land for

CRPF battalions in Delhi because of extra deployment and because there was great movement of this force to and from Punjab as those were the days of terrorism there. I sought an appointment with Bhagat through my Commandant and he called me immediately. He remembered that I had treated him well and helped him in the old days when he was a small-time politician. He warmly greeted me and after tea asked me whether he could do anything for me. I told him about our requirement for land. He immediately rang up the then Vice-Chairman of the Delhi Development Authority (DDA) and we got many plots for the force. I had a similar experience with Sikander Bakht when I was in the Central District. He too was a small-time politician from the Jama Masjid area who later became a minister in the Central government and helped me officially in some matters, not forgetting that I had done the same for him.

Another development took place at that time. One day I was summoned by my IG, L.S. Bisht. It was rather unusual for an IG to call a junior officer and I was worried, thinking that I must have done something wrong again and was being called for a reprimand. When I appeared before him in his office, I was surprised when I heard what I had been called for. He wanted me to shift to a government house allotted to me in the Police Lines in Kingsway Camp as Bharat Nagar was not a place for a senior officer who has to interact with a lot of people. I was told this in one sentence while I was still standing. I answered by saying, 'Yes, Sir', saluted and turned back. How did he know I was living in Bharat Nagar? I wondered about this in my naïve way, but heaved a sigh of relief that I had not messed up anything. Back home, I told my father about the order. He had a hearty laugh and said, 'Now I'm sure you'll obey your IG and move out. When I told you to do so earlier you did not listen to me.'

So, we moved out, with my parents helping us to settle down there. Setting up a house was not that easy. We had to buy some basic things for the household like kitchen items, dining table, almirah, and so on. It was a big flat, called a D-II type, on the first floor, consisting of two big bedrooms with attached toilets, a drawing room and a kitchen. The flat faced the main road of Kingsway Camp. I took the help of the SHO, Kashmere Gate, Mam Chand, who got us the required items at reasonable rates, but I paid through my nose as my salary was not much. I still possess that kitchen almirah, reminding me of those days. For Jyoti, it was a great effort to set up a house but she did it very efficiently. She has always been an excellent house manager and a cook as well as good at managing finances. But for her, we wouldn't have organized our new life reasonably well, especially from the financial point of view.

A short while later, I was allotted one of the newly built bigger flats on the second floor nearby. I was also transferred as the Additional SP, Central District. N.K. Shingal was the SP. He was a thorough professional and I learnt a lot from him. One day, he told me rather casually that his office room looked very shabby, so without telling him, I spent the following weekend getting his room done up, replete with whitewashing, polishing of the entire furniture, and so on. When he came to the office on Monday, he was pleasantly surprised and complimented me after discovering that I had got it done. During this posting, I learnt more about the investigation of cases from him.

On the law and order front, I learnt about the arrangements to be made during the Prime Minister's visit when Mrs Gandhi visited Patel Nagar for one of the election rallies. Then there were huge rallies held on the Ram Lila ground and cricket Test matches at the Feroze Shah Kotla ground, football matches at the nearby Ambedkar Stadium, Muharram processions by the Muslim community, among other huge gatherings of people, where police arrangements had to be made. The district was sensitive from a communal point of view as a sizeable Muslim population was concentrated in Jama Masjid and the adjoining areas. The police had to always be on the alert as occasionally, there were clashes between Hindus and Muslims, but they were usually controlled. During this period, the office of the SP, Central District, had also been shifted from Tis Hazari to Daryaganj in a new building next to the police station.

K.K. Paul, who later became Commissioner of Police of Delhi and Governor of Meghalaya, Manipur and Uttarakhand after that, was one of the IPS probationers attached to the district for training, and I would take him along to learn the ropes, including the inspection of police stations. During that period, a new DIG (Range), S.V. Tankhiwale, an IPS officer of the first batch of 1948, from Maharashtra, joined the Delhi Police. He once took me along to Shahdara in North District where a violent situation had erupted. A Home Guard officer, I think his name was Onkar Singh, was killed due to a love triangle and the police was blamed for not handling the matter well. On 15 and 16 August 1972, the enraged local people started stoning the police station of Shahdara. A battle raged between the police and the locals near the police station. Since Tankhiwale was new to Delhi, he took the incident casually and took me in his car with no force accompanying us to Shahdara, from the Wazirabad side. As soon as we reached the crowd, which was now between the Shahdara police station and us, the crowd looked back and seeing us in uniform as we got out of the car, came towards us menacingly. Just the two of us couldn't do much as we didn't have weapons. The crowd started pushing us towards the police station, punching and even hitting us with lathis. I was injured badly that day. However, once we managed to get inside the police station, we were safe. Somehow, the situation was handled and the locals calmed down, but it took a few days. The press covered the incident, including mentioning the injuries I had suffered.

Another incident, known as the Prem Lata episode, took place in the jurisdiction of a police post in September, 1972 on Tank Road in the Karol Bagh area. An 11-year-old Scheduled Caste girl had committed suicide, I don't recall what for, and people were agitated. They started gathering in large numbers and when the police tried to control them, they became violent. It took almost five to six days to control the situation. We were literally on the road round the clock. I recall once there was a police party present along with me and the highly experienced, 'risen from the ranks' DSP Choudhary Om Prakash. The crowd started marching towards us. Knowing that we were too few in number and would not be able to handle the situation, we decided to retreat. Choudhary Om Prakash said, 'Let us not run back as that will send a bad message. I'll ask the policemen to kneel down in firing positions so that the crowd will expect firing and halt or go back. Then we'll ask the policemen to form a marching squad and move forward a little and then backward as a drill and in that way can make a distance between us and the crowd.' I nodded and that is how some embarrassment was avoided. Choudhary Om Prakash was a stalwart along with Pandit Sham Lal and Bakshi Vishwa Nath who were all SDPOs in the district.

K.K. Paul remembers this episode of Prem Lata's suicide as a training ground since it gave him exposure to the field that day. He reminded me some time ago that I used to take him from the Gazetted Officers' Mess in Kingsway Camp at 6 a.m. every morning and drop him back at about 10 p.m. for those five to six days. He also had the first experience of tear gas that the police had used to successfully avert the burning of buses by rioters.

Meanwhile, another development was taking place. Two more UTs, Manipur and Tripura, were granted statehood on 21 January 1972 and the UT cadre had to be bifurcated again. Earlier, this was done when the UT of Himachal Pradesh had been given statehood in 1971. In the cadre, there was some anxiety about who would be allotted to this new cadre, but we felt that the needful would be done in all fairness. P.R. Rajagopal from the Madhya Pradesh cadre had taken over as the IG, Delhi. I learnt that the government had asked M.G. Pimputkar, an upright Indian Civil Service (ICS) officer who was then the Lieutenant Governor of Delhi, to draw up a criterion for the bifurcation of the cadre and suggest names for postings. The rumour was that he had kept the list of the recommended names in his pocket lest it was leaked out! I thought that the matter was in safe hands and justice would be done. Someone also told me that I was not going to the new cadre.

One day, Gautam Kaul of the 1965 batch, my senior and good friend, phoned me and said, '*Suna hai ke tum Manipur wali list mein daal diye gaye ho* (I have heard that your name has been put in the list of Manipur).' It was a bombshell for me. He has been always well informed because of his connections (his mother Shiela Kaul was a Congress leader) and there was no reason to disbelieve him. I was crestfallen. Later, I came to know that I was not going to the new cadre of Manipur and Tripura and instead, a batchmate of mine figured in the list. The rumour was that my batchmate's wife was from Jammu and knew Om Mehta, also from Jammu, who was a powerful minister then; she got my name exchanged through him. I didn't have any political godfather nor did I know that you needed one. Even if I had known, I couldn't have cultivated one because I had understood that one has to make compromises for such a relationship. But it was clear that gross injustice had been done to me for no fault of mine. I was disgusted at the political machinations.

I had thought that IAS and IPS officers were full of integrity and were dealt with fairly, but I was mistaken. It was not only me but quite a few others were also treated in a similar way. The powerful ones who were selected for the new cadre manipulated the political and higher bureaucratic bosses to get their names replaced. The people who did this injustice were Govind Narain (ICS), the then Union Home

Secretary, and Bishen Tandon (IAS) who was a Joint Secretary in the Prime Minister's Office (PMO) and earlier had a stint as the DC of Delhi. Since Tandon knew many officers from Delhi, he helped his favourites. Surely, many other politicians and bureaucrats also would have used their influence. But ultimately, the buck stopped at Mrs Indira Gandhi who allowed this to happen. This was the loudest signal of the concept of a committed bureaucracy, which led to cracks in its steel frame. Since then, the decline has been rapid not only at the Centre but also in the states. Today, the police and other bureaucrats are at the mercy of politicians and they mostly join hands with them to serve themselves at the cost of their duty and conscience.

Anyway, since I couldn't do anything, I had resigned myself to my fate. But, I didn't want to go to Tripura as that was far away and my father wasn't keeping good health. I had to do something urgently to avoid going there. A numerologist told me that I would be heading west and not east, but I did not believe him. However, his prediction turned out to be true. It so happened that P.A. Rosha, my DIG (Range) in the Delhi Police got promoted and posted as the IG BSF, Jalandhar. I approached him for a posting in Punjab on deputation to the BSF. He agreed and got the proposal cleared from the Ministry of Home Affairs. I took the help of Vineeta Singh, the Sub-Divisional Magistrate (SDM) of the same district I was posted in, to speak to her father L.P. Singh who was then the Union Home Secretary.

Meanwhile, unknown to me, Rajagopal, my IG, was planning to post me as the SP of the newly carved East District in the trans-Yamuna area, but I was unaware of his plans. Once the decks were cleared for the BSF, I sought an appointment with him to request him to relieve me from the Delhi Police so that I could join the BSF in Punjab. When I met him, he got very angry and told me that he was planning to post me to the new district as the SP but since I wanted to leave, he would issue orders straightaway. I was taken aback, not knowing his plans and rued going to him. But the die was cast. That mistake proved very costly for me. Had I stayed in the Delhi Police, he could have got my cadre also changed to the UT one as he was very powerful. This event changed the course of my life. The only consolation is that it was a genuine mistake, but I still can't understand why I was in such a hurry to get relieved. We all commit mistakes in life and I also did so many times in my personal and professional life and later paid for it. I console myself always by saying that after all, I am human and there is something called destiny.

Chapter 5

West and North-East

Before joining as the Deputy Commandant of the 54 Battalion of the BSF in Faridkot, Punjab, I took leave for a month. As I was planning to hand over the government flat in the Kingsway Camp Police Lines, my friend and batchmate R.C. Dembla of the Maharashtra cadre, whose house was nearby, got married and wanted to stay in my flat for a month before taking his bride to Mumbai where he was posted. He also said he would pay the rent for that month to me, the amount I had to pay to the government. I brushed aside his offer and gave him my fully furnished flat to enjoy his honeymoon.

After my leave was over and before moving to Faridkot, I called on K.F. Rustamji, the then Director General (DG) of the BSF, in his office in North Block. He had such an awesome reputation, in comparison to which I was a toddler in the service. But as I entered his room, he got up, shook hands warmly with me, offered me a cup of tea and welcomed me into the BSF. I haven't forgotten that gesture till date and learnt how important graciousness is.

He had raised BSF as a force since he was given the responsibility by the Government of India to raise this border-guarding paramilitary force after the 1965 war with Pakistan. He did a great job by first inducting armed police battalions of the states on the borders with Pakistan, like Punjab, Rajasthan, among others, and then planning recruitment for the force.

In the beginning of 1973, I moved to Faridkot in the severe winter and I was officiating as CO of the unit. Initially, I stayed in a large tent with an attached washroom in the unit. I soon hired a house but stayed there only for two nights as the toilet was far away from the bedroom, in the courtyard, and using it at night was a nightmare. Back at the unit, there was a room with an attached toilet in a corner of a plot that had not been used for ages. I got it cleaned up, made it habitable and moved in with Jyoti and Archana, who joined me later.

The battalion in Punjab to which I was posted was a battalion of the Punjab Police earlier. I learnt a lot about the functioning of the unit, which was almost on the army pattern, which is why the BSF and CRPF were called paramilitary forces.

The land for the unit had been bought from the Maharaja of Faridkot who invited us for lunch to his palace. His purpose was to sell more of his land to the BSF as after Independence, the wealth of the Maharajas and other rulers of the erstwhile princely states had dwindled. They were dependent on privy purses which were also abolished at that time by Indira Gandhi. Many of them had begun businesses of different kinds. I could see that his bad days were almost there. In his dilapidated palace, his ramshackle band of a few musicians played for us. He treated us very kindly and served us lunch in silver plates with his best cutlery and the choicest cuisine to titillate our taste buds, but I realized he would not be able to keep up the grandeur for too long.

Archana was very fond of eating eggs. Once while returning from Jalandhar at night, she kept on crying, demanding a boiled egg. The jawans with me had to bring a shop-owner from his house in the cold winter night to provide the eggs. Another episode I remember is when Dr Rao from Hyderabad joined as the Medical Officer in the unit. The train from Delhi reached Faridkot at midnight and the poor chap was not wearing any warm clothes. He had no idea of the severe winter of north India and of Punjab and was shivering when he alighted from the train. He was quickly brought to the unit, given a few pegs of rum and covered with quite a few blankets. He was also given a heater so that he could sleep in comfort. In the morning when he appeared before me, he said he wanted to resign and go back at once as he could not live in the intensely cold winter. We were able to persuade him to hang on. Years later, I bumped into him in North Block, and he was very happy in the BSF as by then, he had settled well.

One day in May 1973, I got a signal from the BSF headquarters that our battalion should move immediately to Allahabad in UP to put down a revolt by the Provincial Armed Constabulary (PAC). Three battalions of the PAC located in Bareilly, Meerut and Agra had violently protested, demanding better pay, working conditions and the right to form unions. The army had been called in to control it, and the clashes resulted in about 30 policemen, soldiers and civilians shot dead and hundreds arrested. It led to resignation of the Congress ministry in UP headed by Kamlapati Tripathi. The BSF was also called in with a mandate to disarm all other PAC units and take control of the situation in the campus of the units. All leave for the personnel in the BSF battalions tasked to move to UP was cancelled and I was asked to take the unit by a special train at the earliest. We placed a demand for a special train with the railways and I went to nearby Ferozepur to meet the seniormost officer stationed there to ask him to get us the train at once. His instance response was that it would take some time. When I insisted that we were in a hurry, he told me something in reply that I can never forget. He said, 'Sir, I have told the train to come at once, if necessary, through the agricultural fields as the BSF is in a hurry!' We both burst into laughter. Humour in stress situations does help in calming nerves.

Back in the unit in the evening, Subedar Major Balwant Rai came over to my house with a request. He was a very mature man with lots of experience. He told me that eight jawans of the unit would have to be given leave for a week to attend to urgent matters at home. I told him firmly that this could not be done as it would be contrary to the orders from above and there would be a problem if those given leave did not come back on the due date at Allahabad. He told me that one jawan's wife was expecting in a day or two, while the surgery of another jawan's father was slated three days later, and so on. I gave in on the condition that I would hold him accountable if they did not rejoin the battalion on time. He agreed; in fact, he offered to be punished with suspension if his word was not honoured by the jawans going on leave. I decided then to grant leave as a special case, against the orders of the BSF headquarters, but true to the Subedar Major's word, all of them did join a week later at Allahabad.

Once at Allahabad, my battalion was asked to move straightaway to the designated places and disarm the PAC units there. No arrangements had been made for the stay of our men and officers, the grim situation there perhaps being the cause of this. I met the District Magistrate (DM) who said that he would need time to help. He refused to give me a room in the Circuit House on the ground that the place was full. I had no option but to tell my jawans to sleep in the buses given to us for a few nights till other arrangements were made. I have seen such problems faced by the Central forces later on also. The states do requisition these forces but do not make proper arrangements for them although it is their duty to do so. On the third day, we were allotted a school building as accommodation, which made us a bit comfortable. I also stayed there in a room for quite some time. The situation came under control with the help of the BSF and the unit had done quite well in the job allotted to it, keeping a strict vigil throughout.

Once matters settled down, I called Jyoti to Allahabad for a few days. We had a dip in the holy Triveni Sangam, and went sightseeing, taking in historical buildings like Anand Bhawan, the ancestral house of Jawaharlal Nehru. Sometime later a Commandant (CO) was posted in the unit as I was still too junior in service to take up that post. B.N. Bhattacharjee, the CO, joined at Faridkot and came to Allahabad. Meanwhile, I wasn't happy to be in the BSF as there was hardly anything to do. I was missing my police work. My father's health had improved a little, so I decided to ask for a posting to Tripura even though it was far away and sent a signal to that effect to my IG, Shri P.A. Rosha. I had hardly done eight months or so in the BSF. He spoke to me and agreed to my request. A grand farewell was given to me by the officers and jawans of the unit at Allahabad. I was garlanded profusely and my jeep, bedecked with flowers, was pulled with ropes with jawans raising slogans of 'Zindabad' for me. I was overwhelmed. I was told that the reason for this grand farewell was that I was considerate to jawans in granting leave to some of them at Faridkot, as narrated earlier. This was yet another lesson—if you look after your men, they'll respect you and obey your orders.

In September 1973, I left for Calcutta (now Kolkata) by the Kalka Mail along with Jyoti and Archana to Agartala, Tripura. We stayed overnight at a relative's place and on the day after, we boarded the small Dakota aircraft from Calcutta in the afternoon for Agartala. The cost of the ticket I think was Rs 75. We boarded the plane in the hangar itself as the aircraft was so small. Flying low over Bangladesh, it hit many air pockets, scaring many passengers. In the entire region of Bangladesh and North-East India, the rainy season extends from roughly April to October due to its proximity to the sea in the Bay of Bengal, and air pockets are a common feature in that region. We were on our way to a new place and felt some anxiety, not knowing what was in store for us. The North-East seemed to be far away, not only for me but even for the Central government in Delhi. I was surprised by the wording of the wireless message to me from the Ministry of Home Affairs. It was, 'Please report to the Chief Secretary, Assam, Agartala'. Even the ministry didn't know that Assam and Tripura were two different states, that Agartala was the capital of Tripura and Assam had nothing to do with it except that both states were in the North-East. What a colossal ignorance! This neglect of and ignorance about that entire region continued till the dawn of the new century when, at last, some awareness started. In the process, the region has suffered badly.

When the plane landed, the sun was about to set, even though it was only about 4.30 p.m. It was a nondescript small airport with an ancient building. A police jeep was waiting for us there. We had taken only two trunks and two beddings with us. The Sub-Inspector (SI) who had come to receive me said that he would take us to the Circuit House where a room was booked for us. Unlike Delhi, the road did not have any traffic congestion. It was flanked by lush green rows of jackfruit trees, giving the impression that we were passing through a forest. We used to buy jackfruit once a while in Delhi, but here you could pluck these by the dozens without paying a single paisa. In the dimly lit Circuit House, we were directed to the room booked for us. It was a small room with a big mosquito net fixed on the double bed with hardly any space to move about. And soon we saw huge mosquitoes flitting around. We were quite demoralized but had to put up with the situation. I went out to locate the staff to seek help for tackling the mosquitoes.

Next morning, I called on the IG in uniform. In fact, he was an officer of the DIG rank but called an IG. He was B.R Sur, who I had met earlier in Delhi when he was SP (Crime) in Delhi. He told me to wait for my posting for a day or two and soon I got posted as

SP of the CID in Agartala itself. Later, I got a better room in the Circuit House. Jyoti started cooking in the room's kitchenette and we settled down. Two orderlies, Dev Anand from Bihar and Debnath, a local constable, were appointed to help us. Debnath used to look after Archana very well. One day, when I was angry with Archana about something, Debnath scolded me. That day he went home late in the evening after Archana had gone to sleep. We put Archana in the nursery section of a local school where she picked up a bit of Bengali and learnt how to eat fish with bones from her classmates. With Dev Anand, I had an interesting episode. Once, when Jyoti went to Delhi, I asked him whether he knew cooking. He replied in the affirmative, so I gave him a 10-rupee note to buy ladyfingers (*okra*). In the evening he placed a big bowl of ladyfinger curry on the table for my dinner. I was shocked because I was not used to eating ladyfinger curry as Jyoti made it dry or fried. When I asked him why he had cooked such a huge quantity, he said that the entire lot had come for Rs 10 and more of the vegetable was still in the bucket!

It was a new field of work for me as the head of the intelligence unit. There was a lot to learn and do. But first I had to familiarize myself with Tripura. It is a small, landlocked, vividly green hill state in the North-East, occupying an area of about 10,492 square kilometres and its altitude varies from 50 to 3080 feet above sea level. It stretches 184 kilometres from north to south and 113 kilometres from east to west. Geographically, the state is a part of the eastern mountains. It is a low-lying plain pierced by a series of low spurs projecting from the Lushai or Mizo hills. There are six prominent hill ranges running parallel from north to south with an average distance of around 20 kilometres between them. It has a tropical climate and receives a good share of the monsoons roughly from April to September each year. Although landlocked, it is crisscrossed by a large number of short and swiftly flowing rain-fed rivers or rivulets. Its principal rivers, such as the Manu and Feni, flow in the north–south direction and drain into the rivers of Bangladesh. It is surrounded by Bangladesh on the north, south and west. The bordering Indian states of Assam and Mizoram lie to the west of Tripura. It was connected to the rest of India by air and land routes at that time and only now train connectivity has come up, but it is a remote state for Delhi. Agartala is the capital and the main languages spoken are Bengali and Kokborok which is the language of the Tripuris, the main tribe of Tripura. Its total population in 1973 was about 25 lakhs and now about 40 lakhs. The Bengalis constitute about 70 per cent of the population and the rest are tribals like Tripuris, Chakmas, Mogs, among others, who have Mongoloid features.

Economically, it is a poor state and the Bengalis, who had taken over most of the land in the plains, are richer than the tribals. The main occupation of the tribals is *jhum* (slash and burn) cultivation. The state was at least 50 years, if not more, less developed than the prosperous states of India. Similarly, its capital was behind Delhi by many decades. The situation is a little better today.

An ancient historical state, Tripura is mentioned by Hiuen Tsang, the famous Chinese traveller, in his travelogue as a great Bor/Borok kingdom in the east of Bengal, and according to some scholars, this reference points towards Tripura. The state was ruled for about 3,000 years by the kings of the 'lunar dynasty'. The last king of Tripura was Kirit Bikram Kishore Manikya Bahadur who reigned from 1947 to 1949 after which the kingdom was merged with the Indian Union on 15 November 1949.

It is said that during the Mahabharata era, the king of Tripura had taken part in the *Rajasuya* (coronation) of Yudhishtira, the eldest Pandava, and thus the state traces its history to that time. Raja Chitra Yudh had attended the ceremony and Emperor Yudhishtira bestowed the *svetchattra* (a royal white umbrella) as an honour on the Raja of Tripura, which to this day is the chief insignia of the royal family of Tripura. The most authentic document on Tripura's royalty is the *Rajmala* (literally meaning the Garland of Kings), a chronicle of Tripura's Manik dynasty that lists 179 kings.

Due to various events in history, Tripura became a small state. It was still predominantly a state of tribals but when Bengali Hindus were targeted due to communal violence against them at the time of the formation of East Pakistan, many rushed to Tripura for refuge. Also, the king of Tripura was the zamindar of a big chunk of land in what became East Pakistan and many of his subjects there who were Hindus escaped to his kingdom. This led to Hindu Bengalis becoming a majority in the state, taking over land and businesses and converting Tripura primarily into a Bengali state, which the tribals resented.

Reverting to my posting, I toured the length and breadth of the state in my jeep. It was a primitive society, but with the charm of an ancient culture almost untouched by modernity. Sometimes Jyoti also came along with Archana in tow. There was hardly any of the infrastructure that exists in more modernized states. Sometimes I had to cross small rivers by walking on bamboo bridges. People lived a simple life and in the interiors it was common to see men and women bathing and washing clothes together with animals. One day, I noticed a man walking in the jungle and asked my driver, Manik Chakraborty, to ask him where he was going. After talking to him, my driver told me that the man was going to visit a relative who lived faraway and the journey would take him two days on foot. He was carrying rice in a small pot, which he would cook on the way by using water from a rivulet and lighting a fire with wood from the jungle, and then sleep in the jungle itself.

Time had no meaning in Tripura. Once, while on a tour, I reached a river crossing from where my jeep was to be loaded onto a large boat to take us across. But there I saw quite a few vehicles, including a truck, parked. I sent for the Sikh driver and asked him how long he had been there and what the reason was. He told me that the boatman was missing, along with his assistant, for the last two days and that was why he and the others were stuck. The rumour was that the boatman and his assistant had imbibed copious amounts of liquor in the evening three days ago and then passed out. On the wireless, we got through to the local police station and the policeman in charge sent two constables to look for the boatman. Finally, he was traced and brought back. That's how I and the others could cross the river, but it still took us about four to five hours.

One day, my driver asked me, 'Sir, there must be very big bamboo houses in Delhi, isn't it?' I was shocked. How could he think that there were houses made of bamboo in Delhi? But then I realized that he knew only of bamboo houses as bamboo was available in plenty in the state and most houses were built of this material, and there were very few *pucca* (concrete) houses constructed of bricks and cement. I told him that there were no bamboo houses in Delhi, then asked him whether he had ever seen a train. He replied in the negative, saying he had, however, seen planes, but expressed a desire to see a train. Once I went to Kailashahar, a town and district headquarters of the north district of Tripura close to the border with Bangladesh, by jeep, a journey that took about eight hours. I travelled by road, even though there was a flight available from Agartala to Kailashahar in those days for which the ticket was only Rs 35 (unfortunately, these flights were later stopped). The reason was that I wanted to show my driver the train at the Dharam Nagar Railway Station there. He was thrilled and got into the stationary train a few times, jumping in excitement like a kid. At present, the railway network has reached Agartala.

On another occasion, I visited a police station in a remote area. There was a small road leading to that place with beautiful valleys on both sides. After my work there was done, the officer-in-charge asked me to have lunch. When I accepted his invitation, he asked me whether I would like to have rice or *chapatti*s. I asked for *chapatti*s and was surprised to see that all I was served were a few strange-looking *chapatti*s with two onions on a plate. I ate whatever I could, thanked him and then asked him who had prepared the food. He said he had done so himself but since like most people in Tripura, they were rice-eaters, he didn't know how to cook *chapatti*s in the right way.

I was leaving in the afternoon, but he asked me not to venture out because it was time for the only elephant in the region to come onto the road and he would topple my jeep if he saw it. He told me that I could not retreat or go forward when the elephant was standing there as it was a narrow road. He informed me that a week ago, the elephant had hurled an 11-year-old girl down into the valley. I was upset because he should have told me this when I had reached in the forenoon. I had to take a call, knowing that I had to go right then. It was very risky but Jyoti was alone in the Circuit House and in the family way. There were no mobile phones in those days to inform her and there was no landline phone either at the police station. The wireless set at the police station was also not working. I took the risk of going with prayer on my lips, but nothing untoward happened and I reached Agartala safely.

On the work front, an event worth mentioning took place. Mrs Indira Gandhi had visited Agartala as it was a Congress-ruled state and Sukhamoy Sen Gupta was the Chief Minister, a very shrewd politician. As she was alighting from the aircraft, the local Intelligence Bureau (IB) officer handed me over a secret envelope. I opened it a little later only to read that there was a possibility that a black flag demonstration against her would be held at the airport at the time of her arrival. Fortunately, there was none.

Bangladesh had been liberated only about two years before and Tripura had played a very important role during its struggle against Pakistan. Many VIPs and refugees from there had taken shelter in

Tripura, while it was from there that many operations of the Mukti Bahini, the army and the BSF were launched. Since Tripura almost protrudes into Bangladesh, it was well connected with it on the long borders. The people of Bangladesh were friendly towards us, yet showed some hostility against India because of their old links with Pakistan, which is why hatred for India was built into their psyche. The DM and SP of the adjoining districts of Bangladesh often came on official visits to Agartala and vice versa, and both sides made lavish arrangements for the stay of visitors. The Akhaura border checkpost in Bangladesh on the other side was hardly about two kilometres away from Agartala. During this time, Major General J.F.R. Jacob, Chief of Staff of the Eastern Command, who had played a major role in the liberation of Bangladesh, called me one day to Raj Bhavan for a briefing by me on the prevailing situation.

At that time, the migration of Bengali Hindus from Bangladesh into Tripura was continuing and those who had migrated earlier were helping them to come in and settle down as most of them were in government jobs and otherwise well-entrenched in Tripura. It was a porous border and the smuggling in of people and goods was not difficult. I had alerted my immigration staff at the Akhaura checkpost to be very vigilant. One day, my staff was able to catch two young girls who were trying to cross the border with crudely made forged papers. All the four DSPs with me, who were promoted from the ranks and were in their fifties, were Bengali Hindus. They pleaded with me not to hand over these girls to the Bangladesh authorities because they would be raped and converted. I refused to budge. Then they brought these girls to my office and both of them, in a sudden move, fell at my feet crying. It seemed they had been tutored by those officers to plead to be allowed to staying on. I was dumbfounded and told the officers to take them away. It was a catch-22 situation. They had made an illegal entry but the threat to them was real. I gave in by saying that they should consider that the matter had not come to my notice. Otherwise, they would have been arrested or deported, and in case of the arrest, they would have to be produced before a court the next day. Talking of courts, a court one day issued an arrest warrant against an accused who had already gone across to Bangladesh—the logic for the court's verbal order was that if it was so easy to cross the border, the police could also cross it and arrest him from there!

The Communist Party (Marxist) (CPM), led by Nripen Chakraborty and Dasarath Debbarma, was the major Opposition political party then in Tripura. Once it called for a strike among government employees. The IG immediately called all the SPs and told them to ensure that the employees of the police department did not participate in the strike as it would be an insult to the department. I spoke to my entire staff personally, so none of them went on strike, but the employees in all the police offices, including the office of the IG, obeyed the CPM. The government was very angry with the CPM on this and some other issues. One day, Chief Minister Sukhamoy Sen Gupta called many officers to his residence for a meeting and the IG took me along too. The Chief Minister told the IG to arrest Members of the Legislative Assembly (MLAs) of the CPM from the Assembly as the session was on. In bravado, B.R. Sur, my IG, said, 'Sir, we'll smash their heads. Don't worry. The needful will be done.'

On the way back, the IG asked me how to go about it. I had no clue. We needed some kind of criminal evidence against them to pick them up and there was nothing on record. He asked me to fabricate reports against them of plotting criminal activities of different kinds against the state. When I politely refused, he got angry with me. He put my Additional SP, Gon Choudhary, on the job. Gon Choudhary, along with the DM, fabricated source reports against the MLAs and took the decision to arrest them the moment they came out of the Assembly. Somehow, the MLAs got the information that the police were waiting for them, so they didn't come out and the plan failed. In the next elections, the CPM came to power. In the post-Emergency era, when the new anti-Congress governments appointed Commissions of Inquiry against the excesses of the previous governments, including those during the Emergency, the CPM government of Tripura also appointed a Commission of Inquiry headed by Justice Barman from the Orissa High Court. A complaint on this particular case of fabrication of false reports against the CPM MLAs was filed. I was in Delhi then, in the Bureau of Police Research and Development (BPR&D), and summoned to depose as the complaint was against the then SP (CID). I told the Commission truthfully about the above sequence of events. Sur and Gon Choudhary were then called and grilled. Consequently, the Commission complimented me and indicted them.

As I have said earlier, Chief Minister Sukhamoy Sen Gupta was very shrewd. One of his ministers, who was the in charge of relief measures in the state, was creating political problems for him. One day, the Chief Minister summoned me and asked to conduct an inquiry by physical verification into the relief work done on the orders of that minister for which money had been distributed. It was mostly about the wells dug in the state in different areas. I worked hard and went round to the designated places but couldn't find a single well! Nor could I locate any beneficiary whose signature was on the rolls for receiving money for the work done. I handed over the report to the Chief Minister directly as he had ordered, but kept my IG informed. He knew the facts already. He took the report and in my presence locked it in the almirah in his office. I was happy that I had done a good job and expected action against the minister, but nothing happened except that the minister stopped troubling the Chief Minister.

During that period, I wrote an *Intelligence Manual* also. On the personal front, we were allotted a house in Kunjban, the government colony. In addition to the two orderlies, Dev Anand and Debnath, who had worked for us when we were still in the Circuit House, we had Chakraborty, a cook from the Home Guards, who joined us. Once by chance my wife found out that our cook was not eating food during the day in order to save money to send home. We felt bad and Jyoti started giving him rations rather than money and would regularly visit him in his tent outside to see whether he was eating or not. Later, I got him recruited as a constable so that he could get a higher salary. At the time of his recruitment, he wanted Rs 10 to bribe the doctor to clear him in medical examination. But I refused and instead told him that I would speak to the doctor. When he pleaded with me not to do that, my father-in-law, who was there and overheard this conversation, gave him Rs 10 for the purpose.

Jyoti had gone to Delhi for the delivery of our second child. Those were the days of letters and telegrams. I was delighted when I got a telegram from my father-in-law informing me that a daughter had been born. I was able to see the baby after about two months when I went on leave to Delhi. We named her Sonya. When I returned with the family, Jyoti hired a maid to look after our daughters and I named her Hema Malini as we already had Dev Anand at home (after the popular Bollywood stars)! Even now, I call every maid who works in my home Hema Malini!

Sonya, called Sonu at home, was a naughty kid and would often fall from the bed to the floor. It got us worried and special care had to be taken of her. In contrast, Archana, called Achu at home, was docile. I have heard a theory that the first child is always overprotected. By the time the second is born, the parents have enough experience and don't pay attention to small problems of the child who becomes naughty to draw attention and is usually an extrovert. Since Achu was very fond of eggs, we kept a few hens in our compound, and she was thrilled when the first egg was delivered by the hen in her hideout.

While we were in Tripura, many relatives came on visits, so we would take them around to see the places of interest like the Unakoti Caverns and Caves in the north, the Tripura Sundari Temple in the south, Ujjayanta Palace in Agartala, and Neermahal in Melaghar area. Agartala in 1973 was a small town with just one small market and no restaurant worth the name. The shopkeepers used to close their shops for lunch and go home.

We entertained ourselves by a lot of social activity, including formal and informal dinners, especially with the BSF officers there. Jain, a Hindi school teacher from Indore, was our neighbour and he and his good-looking wife were devotees of Sai Baba. We also met Dr Krishan Mohan from Delhi, an orthopaedic surgeon in the local hospital, who was a good doctor and a jovial person.

I was fond of liquor. I also used to smoke occasionally in those days in parties. Soon after I landed in Agartala, when I found out that a bottle of rum cost only two and a half rupees, I bought a whole crate. And I got a bottle of White Horse scotch whisky for Rs 17 from R.K. Dua, a CRPF Assistant Commandant who was posted there. I knew him as I had met him once in train while coming to Calcutta. Later, he worked with me when I went on deputation to the CRPF as a DIG. I hit it off very well with R.C. Kochhar, my senior colleague who was an ex-army officer, a very interesting and brilliant person, with many original ideas on various matters. His only problem was that he was a terror for the subordinates who kept out of his way. Like me, he was fond of liquor.

One day Kochhar invited me to his house and opened his bar made of bamboo with beautiful designs. The bar was lined with all kinds of scotch and other whisky. I was impressed and asked him how he had such a collection at a godforsaken place like Agartala. He told me that he would let me know later. Keeping his promise, he took me to a private house one day and knocked at the door. When a lady opened the door, Kochhar asked her to give whisky bottles to him and she handed over two empty bottles of scotch whisky of different brands. I asked him what was happening but he said that he would tell me after reaching home. Once there, he poured an ordinary Indian whisky in both the bottles, placed them in his bar, and asked me, 'Sir, which whisky will you have?' We both had a big laugh.

Later on, we both were transferred to Delhi and he was to leave a week earlier than me for the Indo-Tibetan Border Police (ITBP) headquarters to which he was posted. The evening before his departure, we went to his house to meet him and saw compact boxes well packed with his stuff. I asked him about the source of these boxes and he told me that he had got these from the Bata Shoe shop in the town. Next morning, when we returned home after seeing him off at the airport, his orderly came to my house with two similar big boxes! What a gesture! There was no way I could thank him immediately as there were no mobile phones and I didn't have his new office phone number at Delhi. I met him only after about two months when I thanked him.

Once I got a letter from home saying that my father was ill and in hospital. It took me about two days to speak to my mother on a trunk call while sitting in the telephone exchange in Agartala to ask her about his condition. She told me that his condition wasn't good. I met the IG and asked for leave. He said yes and I rushed to the airport, leaving my application form behind without his formal sanction. The plane had to be kept waiting for me. In those days it was possible for a police officer to make a plane wait on his orders—a far cry from today. As I was about to board the plane, the IG called me at the airport and asked, 'Where are you?'

'At the airport, Sir. I'm going to board the plane.'

'But your leave has not been granted,' he said and disconnected the phone.

I was flabbergasted and didn't know what to do. I had to make a quick decision. I went ahead. At Calcutta, I met I.M. Mahajan, DIG

CRPF, who was in the Delhi Police earlier and sought his advice. He told me to go back to Agartala, get my leave formally sanctioned as otherwise Sur may take disciplinary action against me. I did that. When I met him after returning, the IG just smiled and I couldn't help feeling anger at his insensitivity.

I came to Delhi after getting my leave sanctioned and later, decided to ask for a posting on deputation due to my father's health. Unfortunately, the Chief Minister did not forward my name for deputation at the behest of Sur. But I kept seeking help elsewhere. R.K. Ohri, the AD in the BPR&D, came to Agartala for some official work along with a colleague. I knew him from my Delhi Police days as he was the SP there. I asked him to help me in getting a deputation and he did so, as his organization needed officers. Still the Chief Minister did not relieve me. I sought the help of Gautam Kaul, my senior colleague from Delhi. His mother Shiela Kaul was a senior Congress leader (they are related to the Nehru/Gandhi family) and she got me relieved in May 1976. At the last minute also, Sur tried to stop me from getting a posting to Delhi but didn't succeed.

Over all, it was not a bad experience serving in Tripura—getting to see nature at its best, dealing directly with politicians for the first time, interacting with simple people, and witnessing high rate of poverty as well as unemployment, and lack of development in a neglected part of India. It was an exposure that helped me professionally.

Chapter 6

Back to Delhi

In Delhi, I joined the BPR&D in May 1975. The office was in a rented building in Safdarjung Development Area. Though happy to be back in Delhi primarily to look after my ailing father, logistics became a problem. Getting a government house in Delhi at that stage of service was difficult, so I was staying at Bharat Nagar in my parents' house in north Delhi, my original home. Transport was another problem. No government jeep or car was provided as this organization was nascent and perhaps considered less important than other governmental organizations. There was just one car available, only for the Director. I became an office *babu* once again, going to work in a chartered bus with my tiffin box in hand for lunch.

To reduce the commuting time, my wife and I looked for a flat on rent nearby but couldn't afford the rent. Luckily, someone told me that I could soon get a one-room flat in the transit hostel accommodation for government officers at Curzon Road (now Kasturba Gandhi Marg) which has quite a few such flats in multi-storeyed buildings. The very next day, I went to the Estate Office and got a ground floor apartment in B Block. To our relief, at least one problem was solved as my travelling distance was cut down by at least half. After a few months doing research work in my organization, I was posted as the AD (Administration). To make life easier, I started looking for an office space for the BPR&D near my flat. God must have noticed my wish because a few days later, as I was out for a walk in a lane just outside the hostel premises, I saw an old barrack-type government building being vacated. I promptly made inquiries, went to the Estate Office and got it allotted for the office. After some renovation work, the office was shifted there and my office commute became a few minutes' walk from my flat. What could be a bigger luxury than that in a big city like Delhi!

I was quite happy with the work I had to do. There was a lot to do on the administrative side. Three Central Forensic Science Laboratories and three Central Detective Training Schools in Calcutta, Hyderabad and Chandigarh were part of the BPR&D, and I had to visit these occasionally for work. Dr S. Venugopal Rao of the Andhra cadre, a scholarly man, was the Director. K.K. Dave was number two in the organization as well as in charge of the training division. S.K. Malik was an IG located at Calcutta to look after the forensic labs. I had a good rapport with officers like T.G.L. Iyer, Deputy Director, and T.R. Kalra and B.R. Luthra, both ADs. I learnt a lot from these good souls, who enjoyed laughter along with their drinks. Unfortunately, they both have left for heavenly abode.

Soon after we shifted to the new office at Curzon Road, Prime Minister Indira Gandhi imposed an Emergency in the country on 25 June 1975 after she lost an election petition in the Allahabad High Court. With subsequent support from the Supreme Court, she assigned many extraordinary powers to herself. She locked up all the leaders of the Opposition and anyone else who did not support her. Of the many stories of atrocities by the then Central government across India, especially Delhi, the compulsory sterilization of men for checking the population growth, the atrocities in the Turkman Gate area against Muslims, dismal jail conditions for people like the Maharani of Jaipur, who were imprisoned for speaking against the government, made headlines. Many, including Babu Jagjivan Ram, a senior Dalit leader, left the Congress Party. Everyone was affected, one way or the other.

On the personal front, we had opened a post office savings account for Rs 20 per month each for Archana and Sonya as we felt we would need money for their higher education and weddings later. We couldn't afford more than that, but this amount was considered sufficient then. At that time, the girls got admission in Presentation Convent School near Red Fort with great difficulty and with the intervention of our connections in the police. For Sonya, there was another interesting episode before her admission there. Since she was younger than Archana, we decided to put her in Bharatiya Vidya Bhavan across the road. But my wife and I failed in the interview held by the BVB for her admission! Whereas the august UPSC had selected me for the IPS, this school rejected me! I spoke to the local SHO who promptly went to the school, completed her admission formalities and deposited the fees. Later, Sonya went to another private school at Hailey Road run by a foreigner and then to Presentation Convent School.

Meanwhile, my father's health was deteriorating and Parkinson's disease was making his disability worse with the passage of time. He was admitted many times in G.B. Pant Hospital under the care of Dr S. Janaki, the renowned neurologist and the sister of the famous cardiologist, Dr S. Padmavati. My civilian office gave me enough time to look after him. I was lucky to have Constable Birbal from the Delhi Police as my orderly on deputation to the BPR&D. Besides, the Delhi Police was kind enough to give me the part-time services of a sincere head constable to look after my father during the days he was admitted there. Financially, it was a difficult period and I had to take a loan of

Rs 1,600 from my life insurance policy for his treatment. Ultimately, he passed away in July 1976, which was a huge emotional blow to me. For his cremation and related expenditures, my cousin K.K. Vohra chipped in financially. Till date I remain beholden to him for this help. Of course, it was nice of him to say that my father was his uncle also and he had done no favour. Later, when I could afford to return the money, he flatly refused to take it.

Office work was going on smoothly for some time, but my bad stars emerged after a while. M.L. Bhanot of the UT cadre, whom I had known from my Delhi Police days, joined as the DIG and, therefore, was my boss. God knows for what reason he didn't like me and started making my professional life miserable. He would comment adversely on my work and even make fun of the clothes I used to wear. Adding to my misfortune, Shrawan Tandon, who had also served in the Delhi Police as his boss, joined our office as the head. Though a very good man, he was very fond of Bhanot and this created problems for me with another colleague joining hands with them as well. Of course, Bhanot was a very competent and bold officer. I would like to narrate an incident of his boldness. Once, he told me that our office timings should start at 10 a.m. and not at 9.30 a.m. like the ministries of the Government of India. I told him that since ours was a departmental office, it had to open half an hour earlier in accordance with the government rules. He told me to draft a letter to the Ministry of Home Affairs, suggesting the change in timings, stating that if no reply was received by the end of that month, we would presume that the ministry had agreed to our proposal. When this paperwork was complete, he asked me to hand over the letter meant for the ministry to him. When I gave it to him, he tore it into pieces and threw it into the dustbin. Naturally, since no reply came from the ministry by the end of the month, we changed the office timings!

During this period, I was summoned to Agartala by the Justice

Barman Commission of Inquiry to appear in a complaint against me by the CPM there for fabricating source reports against them of subversion when I was the SP of the Crime CID, an incident I have mentioned earlier. The CPM had come into power in Tripura in this period just after the Emergency, as the Central government and many state governments had changed due to the elections held then. The Congress Party lost heavily and the Janata Party, a coalition of the Opposition parties that merged to form this party, took over at the Centre with Morarji Desai as the Prime Minister. Commissions of Inquiry were set up at the Centre (the Shah Commission) and by many state governments to inquire into excesses committed during the Emergency.

I had become entitled to air travel by then as I had got my selection grade, but on the advice of DIG Bhanot, who wanted to harass me, our Director did not allow me to travel by air on the grounds of economy, which was patently against the rules. However, I appeared before the Commission at Agartala and was cleared of the charges as the signatures on the fabricated reports were not mine—they were signed by the then Additional SP. Justice Barman of the Orissa High Court complimented me for taking a stand and saying 'No' when I was asked to fabricate the source reports against the CPM MLAs there.

I was having a very difficult time due to my equation with DIG Bhanot and was mulling options, but nothing was working out. But then S. Tandon, our Director, was called back to UP, his cadre, and P.R. Rajagopal, my erstwhile boss in the Delhi Police, who had also led the investigative team on complaints in the famous Shah Commission, came to the BPR&D as the new Director. After some days, when he had settled down, I decided to take a big risk and complain to him about Bhanot. Since he knew me well, I bit the bullet, even though I realized that it could boomerang and I risked being thrown out of the organization for complaining against my boss. Rajagopal also knew a bit about Bhanot but verified the contents of my verbal complaint from T.G.L. Iyer, the other DIG, who corroborated my version. I was sitting in my room, very nervous, and keeping my fingers crossed at my action and that too in a uniformed service like the police. I was preparing myself mentally to go to Tripura on repatriation and even be subjected to disciplinary action for lodging a complaint against my boss. Later I was told that after corroborating my version of his behaviour towards me, Rajagopal called Bhanot to his office, gave him a dressing down and asked him to leave the organization at once. That was the end of my ordeal but it was a matter for which Bhanot never forgave me. He still got my Annual Confidential Report (ACR) from Tandon spoiled but luckily, the adverse report was overridden by Rajagopal. Thank God, I was saved by the skin of my teeth!

Reverting to my BPR&D days, financially it was a very difficult time. By the 25th or so of every month there would be no money at home. One evening, Kulbir Singh, two years my senior in the Delhi Police who had helped me get my first promotion and had been a close friend since then, came to meet us with his wife. Being very informal, he told me that he would like to have butter chicken for dinner. It was the last week of the month. My wife and I exchanged despairing glances as we didn't have even Rs 22 to buy butter chicken from the Minar restaurant in Connaught Place. However, Birbal, our orderly and man Friday, heard the conversation and asked us not to worry. He then bought it from the restaurant by paying from his own pocket. Birbal was always a great help. When he died recently, we both went over to his village in Haryana to pay homage to him.

While in the BPR&D, I edited the Police Research and Development (R&D) journal, wrote a few articles and started writing my first book, a novel, *The Thorns*, on the functioning of the criminal justice system in India. In the plot, a girl is kidnapped and raped, but ultimately the accused is acquitted. It was published in 1983 by renowned publisher

Arnold-Heinemann, and its cost was Rs 15. This was followed by quite a few books by me later on.

One day, my Director, Rajagopal, asked me to go to the Foreign Post Office at Bahadur Shah Zafar Marg to pick up a package containing artificial limbs for a child who had lost his arms due to electrocution. Rajagopal had ordered the package from the USA but the post office was not releasing it. He handed me a piece of paper on which all the details were written. I went to the post office and met I.S. Narula of the Indian Postal Service, who was senior to me in service and the boss there. Those were the days when you couldn't import even a needle from abroad without an import licence and these limbs had been imported without one. When I asked him to let me have the package, he flatly said 'No'. I told him, 'Sir, you are an important officer. It is a question of the life of a child. If a tiny violation of rules takes place without any mala fide intention and which can improve the life of a disabled child, it is worth it. After all, if everything is to be done in accordance with rule books, then officers are not needed. Only clerks are sufficient.'

That hit him. He handed over the parcel to me. I returned and gave it to my boss while the person who had perhaps requested it was in Rajagopal's office. Must be an old friend of the boss, I thought.

Rajagopal was succeeded by H.R.K. Talwar of the Haryana cadre as the Director and I was sent on a three-month training course to London at the Royal Institute of Public Administration in the summer of 1980 under the Colombo Plan. It was a dream come true as it was a rare thing for IPS officers to go abroad on courses then. I was quite excited. I got merely 20 pounds before boarding the British Airways flight. When the plane landed in Dubai for a halt en route, I noticed the passengers getting down hurriedly. I felt that something had gone wrong and also got up to move quickly towards the exit gate. Outside, I realized that they were all moving fast to buy duty-free goods as

Dubai was considered cheap. I also bought a pair of binoculars for eight pounds. Later, just when the plane was landing at Heathrow Airport, I was thrilled to see the landscape and houses with red-tiled slanting roofs.

After deboarding, the difficulty started as I was not used to carrying my own bags. I had no option but to walk with my luggage to a designated spot at some distance where somebody was to pick me up and drop me at my hotel, which was near the Euston metro station. At the hotel, the receptionist asked me to pay eight pounds for one day's rent in advance. I had only 12 pounds and was reluctant to part with eight more as I would have been left with only four pounds. I had already spent eight pounds on the binoculars in Dubai, which I repented. But the receptionist didn't relent and informed me that my breakfast next morning was included in the rental. That was a relief. I had to go to the British Council office the next morning and was worried whether a cab would take me there for four pounds! Anyway, I moved to the room that had no attached toilet and I had to go to the washrooms in the lobby which were shared with others.

Next morning, considering the shortage of money, and as I was also excited about the London metro, I decided to use it to go to the British Council office. Not knowing that there are different lines going to different destinations, I got onto the first one I saw after buying the ticket. After a while, I wondered whether I had boarded the right train and when I asked someone, he told me that indeed I was on the wrong metro line. I changed lines and managed to reach the office where Elizabeth, the host from the Council, was waiting for me and others. An amiable, warm-hearted British girl, she made me feel comfortable after I told her my woes. She said that I should have hired a cab because she would have paid after I had reached. Anyway, she gave me a good amount of the allowance money due to me under the scheme, making me feel secure. I was told that I could stay in the hotel for a few days, but later I should manage expenses within the allowance I was given. I realized that I could not afford the hotel on a long-term basis.

Our class consisted of two more Indians, one from the Indian Revenue Service (IRS) and the other, a lady, from the Indian Postal Service. Others were from different countries of Africa, three from Iran, one from Indonesia, etc. In all, we were about 30 officers. David Hall was the course director. I enjoyed the classes and my visit to London. I spent the evenings roaming around the city with a map in hand and became quite conversant with it. Many sights overawed me.

I think many Indians would like to go to England at least once as we and, indeed, a large part of the world were ruled by the British so we were curious about them. Seeing shops like the Harrods department store in Knightsbridge and the famous Oxford Street was another eye-opening experience as it was an ultimate shopping paradise. Once I was invited by an Indian contact for dinner and while seeing me off at the metro station, he forced me to get into the metro without a ticket. I was scared of being caught travelling ticketless, but fortunately, nothing happened. When I got down at my station, I noticed a separate queue of people, who couldn't buy tickets at the entry point, waiting to pay in cash while exiting. This showed discipline. I also stood in the queue.

My colleague from the IRS and I rented an apartment in the Finchley area of London. The work was divided between us. He could cook and I took on the responsibility of washing dishes. On the very first day, I offered to make tea, but when I put the water in a saucepan on the gas stove, I noticed that it took a long time to heat. Perplexed, I asked him what the problem could be as he had been living in the apartment earlier too. He said that the electricity was probably cut off as we must have consumed the quantum of electricity we had paid for. He accompanied me downstairs to put a 50 pence coin in the electricity meter but with no success. Eventually, we had to take the help of the landlady to use this device. All in all, it took more than half an hour for two cups of tea to be made!

Being a policeman, I was keen to see the working of the police and visited a police station after the formalities. I was surprised to see that they did not follow the systems we observed in India, like the maintenance of a daily diary. When I asked them to show me the barracks for the police station staff, they were surprised and told me that there are no barracks. Instead, they had a section house with separate rooms for each policeman. Things like keeping a daily diary and barracks had been given to us by the British but they had themselves dispensed with these. However, they were basically like us in India as far as the behaviour of the police goes in many ways.

As a part of our practical work, we were taken to Cardiff in Wales where we were divided into groups of three and given a problem each to solve. I was attached with a hospital which had a system of day care of senior citizens whom the hospital ambulances would ferry from and take back to their homes in the evening. The problem our group had to solve was that the elderly people eligible to use this facility outnumbered the ambulances. So, a solution was to be worked out without spending any additional money. We were able to propose, after studying each case, that some of the persons using this facility could be taken off as they had recovered, and new ones could avail of this facility in their place. The hospital was happy with this suggestion and worked on it.

An unbelievable incident happened during that time in London. As whisky in the market was very expensive, one day I went in the forenoon to India House, the Indian High Commission, with the intention of getting a few whisky bottles since liquor for diplomats is comparatively cheaper. I had decided to walk into the chamber of the First Officer, introduce myself and tell the person what I needed. The first two rooms on the ground floor were locked. The third being open,

I knocked and walked in. I greeted the officer sitting on the chair and introduced myself. To my utter surprise, he got up and walking towards me said, 'Sir, how are you here?' I didn't recognize him and told him that I didn't think we had ever met. 'Sir, we have met. My name is Vinay Agnihotri from the Madhya Pradesh cadre. You had brought artificial limbs for my son from the Foreign Post Office in Delhi when I was sitting with Mr Rajagopal who was my boss in Madhya Pradesh. He had helped me a lot in that matter and so did you. He is the one who got me this posting so that I could get the best treatment for my son. Since he didn't introduce us, you will not remember, but I can never forget you.'

I was amazes at the coincidence of bumping into a person I had helped years later on an unknown day and time in a foreign land! How do you explain that? And because I had helped him, in return, he saw to it that I got my required supply of whisky. In life, such things do happen inexplicably.

My wife joined me in London after about two months and even though she was in the family way, we made a trip to Europe after my course was over, on Eurail Passes, which cost us 102 pounds each in those days. I had saved money for this trip by not having lunch for almost three months, except for a light salty snack I had taken with me from Delhi. Since there was no European Union at that time, I had to get our visas and currency for each country from London. Amounts of each currency we bought in London were stashed away in separate envelopes for our convenience. We used to spend two nights in the train to save travel time and hotel bills and on the third day, we would check into a hotel for a bath and to wash clothes. Every day, we would be in a different city. Starting with Paris, we went to Geneva, Rome, Venice, Vienna, Amsterdam and few other places. In Rome, we could see the Pope during his weekly public appearance, did a lot of sightseeing and ate local food. We faced quite a few problems due to language as at most places, the locals did not speak English, some even deliberately, it seemed. Once, we missed a train connection due to this problem, which landed us in some difficulty as we stopped in Venice by default, instead of Vienna, our intended destination (not a bad outcome although). All in all, it was an enjoyable trip to London and Europe. However, I had started feeling homesick after about two months and wanted to come back. When we landed at the Delhi airport, I was so emotional that I bent down and kissed the earth of my motherland soon after getting down from the aircraft, at the airport itself.

Thereafter, my third daughter Manika was born on 19 November 1980 (a birthday that she shares with Indira Gandhi and later, when she got married, with her mother-in-law), in Willingdon Hospital, now known as Ram Manohar Lohia Hospital, New Delhi. When we were thinking of a name for the newborn, we were reminded of our neighbour, Wing Commander (Retd) Kanwar. He had many money plants in his house and when I asked him the reason, he replied that since he had no money, he kept money plants in the hope that one day real currency would grow on them! Since I was financially in the same league, we decided to call our little daughter Manika in the hope that more money would come our way! But God has his own ways. Instead of more money, Manika took us to Manipur on a transfer! To be honest, like the first two girls, Manika also brought good luck for us. After my wife conceived her, we went to London, I bought my first car, though second-hand, and I was promoted as a DIG although posted to Manipur. These girls have been very lucky for us all through and the run continues till date. May God bless them.

Since the insurgency situation in Manipur was volatile, the state government asked for officers who were on deputation to be posted to the state. Those who had godfathers managed to stay back, but a few people like me got caught. I tried to get a posting to Tripura since

I had served there earlier, but this didn't work out. I finally handed over charge in the BPR&D in the summer of 1981 and packed up to go to Manipur. Since my first two daughters were going to school, we decided to leave them behind with my in-laws in Delhi. Another reason was that the school-going children of government officials in Manipur were not safe. Some days before my departure, a bomb was thrown at a school bus in Imphal by the insurgents, so we knew we could not risk taking them with us.

Chapter 7

Insurgency in the Land of Ras Lila

Jyoti, Manika and I boarded the Indian Airlines flight to Imphal from the Delhi airport, with two suitcases in tow. In those days, that was the only government-owned airline operating most of the flights in the country and had a virtual monopoly due to the policies of protection. You may be surprised to know that the flight took as long as a flight to London from Delhi—almost nine hours! It had four stops en route at Lucknow, Patna, Bagdogra and Guwahati. It was an early morning flight and we landed at the Imphal airport at about 2 p.m., after flying over the lush green landscape with gentle hills stretching all the way from Guwahati. To our pleasant surprise, a cool breeze greeted us as soon as we alighted. Little did I know that Manipur was like a centrally air-conditioned expanse! Moreover, it was a totally different world with its unique scenery of undulating hills, valleys, large lakes and dense forests as well as communities with different rich cultures and laid-back charm almost untouched by economic development.

At the airport, an officer with Mongoloid features in an olive green uniform, along with a few of his men was waiting for me, holding up a placard. I was surprised to see an army officer there to receive me, but I guessed that my temporary accommodation may have been booked in an army Mess. I walked over to him and after introducing myself, asked whether anyone from the Manipur Police had come to receive me. He said that he was from the Manipur Police! I asked, 'How come you are wearing an army uniform?' He replied that in their state, the armed police force had been wearing olive green uniforms for more than a century and that the practice had continued.

We were taken to the Mess of the Second Battalion of Manipur Rifles and saw only a few *pucca* (concrete) buildings en route from the airport, but beautiful scenery. The next day, I reported for duty in uniform to the then IG of Manipur, H.C. Almeida, an officer from Maharashtra on deputation. The police chiefs were always officers on deputation in those days as were some Chief Secretaries. Then he told me the good news that I was being promoted as a DIG and my orders would be issued by the government that evening. I was delighted! When the evening orders came, I was glad to see that I was posted as the DIG (Range). The year was 1981 and I was the first in my batch to become a DIG. The gaps in the promotion of different batches in different states were so stark that when I attended a conference as a DIG after some time later in Delhi, an officer of the 1962 batch from Gujarat also attended it as an SP, a lower rank. My two further promotions as IG and DG of Police also took place in Manipur when I reported there each time after completing my deputation.

An olive green station wagon was given to me as my official vehicle. Flying a flag with a one-star plate and some additional load of brass on my shoulders was a joy and a big responsibility too. Manipur was passing through a very difficult time due to insurgency, so much so that even the capital town of Imphal witnessed firing by separatist groups at security forces almost every evening. The guns used to boom in loud explosions, shattering the silence of the valley.

Let me first talk a little about Manipur. This lush green small state is known worldwide for its famous floating Loktak Lake, the unique Sangai deer, the *Ras Lila* (dance drama of Lord Krishna) and many local festivals and games (polo is Manipur's gift to the world). Manipur lies beyond the Ganges and the Brahmaputra rivers on the North-East frontier of India. Most of the state is covered by undulating hills with a valley in the centre. It is bounded by Myanmar on the east, Assam on the west, Nagaland on the north, and Mizoram on the south. At the time of my first posting to Manipur, the state was connected by air only but now it has a decent train connectivity. The state's total population was 14 lakhs then and now it is just over 31 lakhs. It has a pleasant climate round the year with ample rain between April and October. It is inhabited by Meiteis, mainly Hindus who live primarily in the valley in Imphal and around, Kuki tribes in the extended plains towards Churachandpur, and Naga tribes in the hills, mostly the Tankhgul tribe, each showcasing a unique rich culture. The latter two groups are Christians. Historically, it was ruled by a Maharaja till it merged with the Indian Union on 21 September 1949. It always had a feud with Burma (now called Myanmar) and was a battleground of the British with the Japanese during the Second World War. Colonel Shaukat Malik of Subhas Chandra Bose's Indian National Army (INA) had hoisted the national flag for the first time on the Indian soil on 14 April 1944 at Moirang on the outskirts of Imphal.

The people of all the communities are pleasant-looking and friendly. The Meiteis and the Nagas always felt that they belonged to independent countries and even during the British Raj were given quite a bit of freedom, except for the presence of a British representative. They dreamt of a homeland separate from India and this was the reason why insurgent groups were so active here. The Meiteis had the United

National Liberation Front (UNLF) formed in November 1964, the People's Liberation Army (PLA), the People's Revolutionary Party of Kangleipak (PREPAK), and the Kangleipak Communist Party (KCP). Kangleipak is the ancient name of Manipur. The Nagas formed the National Socialist Council of Nagaland (NSCN) and two other groups later on. These separatist groups were posing a big challenge to the government. Whereas Meitei groups were active in the valley, the NSCN was active in the hills in Ukhrul district adjoining Nagaland. All these groups carried out guerrilla warfare. Apart from a vigorous response by the forces, the Centre and the state government had no other policy in place to meet the challenges posed by these groups.

For the Centre, the North-East was too far from the heart of Delhi and the only action was to send money and forces, the main contact point being a Joint Secretary in the Ministry of Home Affairs. The Central government had rather a cavalier approach to the states and their representatives. I have witnessed Chief Minister Rishang Keishing returning to the state after waiting in vain in Delhi for days together to meet the Union Home Minister. Finally, he was asked to meet the Home Secretary, so I fixed his appointment, but disappointingly, the same time slot was given the next day to the Chief Minister of UP, at his convenience! I realized then that what really mattered was the political strength of a state.

I noticed a similar biased, indifferent attitude later, when I was the DGP of Tripura. I had to meet the Joint Secretary dealing with provisioning to request him to give me just 500 AK-47 rifles for the Tripura police. To my chagrin, he refused to do so, citing a shortage of these weapons. For him, the priority was the state of UP as at the same time, he ordered the release of the same weapons for UP in thousands even though the state was not facing an insurgency. And as far as any action by the state government in the North-East is concerned, the politicians were generally more interested in votes and money, and seemed to be okay with the situation. The bureaucracy has mostly been going through the motions. A big chunk of the funds being sent from the Centre are going to these so-called insurgents in various ways and it suits them to keep the pot boiling.

Ideally, to contain violence by insurgent groups in such situations, the first step taken should be to let the local police lead the operations. However, all the combat in Manipur, when I joined, was left to paramilitary and military forces, with the local police almost missing from huge areas in the state. Actually, this is a failed model where the army and other external forces have not been able to sort out insurgency in more than four decades. The modus operandi should be reversed by strengthening the local police in a big way and withdrawing the army, the Assam Rifles and other armed forces from Manipur as was done in Tripura later with great success. There is no insurgency in Tripura now and even the Armed Forces Special Powers Act (AFSPA), giving sweeping powers to the army with no accountability for atrocities, has been entirely withdrawn from the state. Even though the Modi government repealed AFSPA from several districts across Assam, Nagaland and Manipur from 1 April 2022, I feel complete withdrawal from the North-East will take time.

Reverting to my story, the immediate challenge to the police when I began my work as the DIG in Manipur, was to contain violence and firing by the insurgent groups at security forces. The insurgents had become so emboldened with their success in the outskirts of Imphal that they moved right into the city and would regularly indulge in firing, laying landmines and launching other attacks, leading to loss of lives, especially in the security forces. From our residence in Imphal, we could hear the firing of guns every evening. Once, some policemen were blown up by a landmine from a place very close to where I lived. It is not as if the police and other forces operating there had no success. They did have an upper hand many times in encounters with the separatists, but the violence was not abating. There was so much tension in the air that any loud sound could cause an overreaction. One evening, when I had some senior officers from Delhi as guests for dinner at my residence in the Lamphel area, we heard sudden gunfire in the compound of my bungalow. We all jumped from our chairs, thinking that terrorists had attacked. To our relief, Dev Raj, my Nepali orderly, came in swiftly and said, '*Saab, ek saanp achanak nikal aya tha. Guard ne uspar goli chala di* (Sir, the guard had fired at a snake that had suddenly slithered into our compound).' So all was well but my guests were shattered. I am sure they didn't enjoy that evening much.

The counter-insurgency operations were being led by local police officers and IPS officers as well as the army, Assam Rifles and the CRPF. Among the local competent officers, I would like to especially mention Karunamaya Singh and Romen Kumar Singh, daredevil officers posted as the SP and Additional SP, respectively, of Imphal district. During this period, D.N. Barua joined as the Chief Secretary. I had worked with him in Tripura earlier where he was the Principal Secretary (PS) to the then Chief Minister. Together with him and others, it was decided as a strategy to establish police posts manned by Manipur Rifles in various localities (called *leikai*s in Manipuri), from where the insurgents were operating. The idea was to enter their territory and confront them there. This led to tremendous firing in these posts. However, the ready retaliatory onslaught by Manipur Rifles slowly but surely impelled the insurgents to move out of Imphal as they couldn't confront it every day. But, the battle continued.

A sad part was that I had to attend the cremations of many police personnel killed in encounters with insurgents in Manipur and later in Tripura. Sometimes the number of dead was large, causing much anguish. The saddest scenes were when the next of the kin of the dead would cling to me in grief. Standing in uniform and trying to give them solace in such situations was rather tough.

Although I was busy in the day, there was nothing much to do at home in the evening as there were no TVs in those days, only transistors that broadcast national news, and mostly there was no electricity either. I was staying in the Lamphel area of Imphal city, a place that people in a lighter vein would call 'Lamp Fail'!

On the crime front, there was not much activity and it was managed well by the district SPs. Two among these were fine young IPS officers, Avdhesh Mathur and Amitabh Mathur of Churachandpur and Chandel districts, respectively. However, when I had to tour the districts mostly to oversee the forces' operations, I was always accompanied by many security personnel, with jeeps in the front of my vehicle and at the back in which jawans carrying the latest weapons kept vigil. During my touring, I visited the famous Moreh town in Chandel district in southern Manipur on the border with Burma (now Myanmar), where Amitabh Mathur was the SP. It was a fairly busy place where some official but mostly unofficial trade of items such as drugs, precious stones and Burmese teakwood was conducted. This place is the route to India and onwards for drugs from the Golden Triangle area where the borders of Thailand, Laos and Myanmar meet. This is a centre of a thriving opium economy and a crucial source of narcotics for the world.

I recall one incident that happened in Senapati district in the north of Manipur bordering Nagaland. A Naga village girl was raped and a crowd had gathered to demand justice for the victim. I was rushed to the spot by my IG. Once there, I found out that in accordance with the customary laws of the Naga community, negotiations with the accused party were going on. This ultimately led to a fine of two *mithun*s or *gayal*s (a type of domesticated bovine found in that region) and the matter was settled. So no police case was pursued and I realized that the Nagas have been following these traditions for centuries.

Reverting to Imphal, when some of us had gathered together one evening in the house of an officer, we could hear unusually loud gunshots. An inquiry revealed that 22 terrorists had escaped from the jail they were incarcerated in through a tunnel dug from the toilet of a barrack to the outside. The firing was by the CRPF personnel guarding the jail. I rushed to the jail premises and was given some more details of the incident. The state government was in a soup as Union Home Minister Giani Zail Singh was going to visit Manipur the next morning. I had already been detailed to go to Tamenglong, a district headquarters in western Manipur, where the minister would arrive by a helicopter the next day. An officer of the DIG rank was IG (Prisons) at the time of the incident. I had a hunch that I would perhaps get posted in his place and even told my wife, as she happened to be in Imphal those days. I left for Tamenglong the next morning. Believe me, it took almost six hours to cover a distance of about 40 kilometres from the highway to this district headquarters in the interior as the road was almost non-existent. My Ambassador car was a big draw as people there hadn't seen that kind of vehicle there ever.

Soon after the Home Minister landed, M.L. Kampani, Additional Home Secretary of the Government of India, whom I knew and who had accompanied the minister, told me that I had been posted as IG (Prisons), a decision the state cabinet had taken last night. My hunch had come true. He said that the state government had faith in me even though there were police officers senior to me in the state. When breakfast was served to the Home Minister, also present at the table were M.L. Kampani, my wife and I, the DM and the SP of the district. Gianiji noticed my wife was wearing *salwar kameez* and understood at once that she was a Punjabi. When he asked her in Punjabi what she was doing there, she replied that her husband was posted to Manipur, indicating who I was with a gesture. Then he asked an officer of the Sashastra Seema Bal (SSB), a Sikh called Jagtar Singh, who was standing close by, whether peace would return to Manipur. When Jagtar Singh said he didn't think so, Gianiji said, 'Okay, then I'll just have my breakfast and leave'—a rustic response from a diehard politician from Punjab!

I took charge as IG (Prisons) and was assisted by two excellent officers of the SP rank, Shyamanand Singh and Karanjit Singh, both on deputation, and all of us worked very hard to tighten the security arrangements and streamline the administration of the main jail from which jailbreaks were not infrequent.

During this period in 1982, I had to accompany my father-in-law to London for a bypass surgery by Egyptian cardiologist Dr Magdi Yacoub, who was famous for conducting such surgeries and, therefore, expensive as his fee for this surgery was 1500 pounds, a huge amount at that time. He successfully operated on my father-in-law a week later in Cromwell Hospital which was very well organized. Although my mother-in-law and I were not allowed to stay in the hospital room allotted to my father-in-law, the staff took exceptional care of him.

On the professional front, I noticed how inclusive and flexible the British police force was when I saw Asian police personnel for the first time on the streets of London. (This was not the case when I had earlier visited the place in 1980 for a training.) Following the 1981 Brixton riots, the government had decided to recruit ethnic minorities into the police force. They changed their rules quickly to improve workforce diversity.

On my return to Imphal, I again plunged into the work of improving the security of the main jail. We dismissed some staff, recruited people and tightened supervision of inmates. We also segregated the insurgents and moved them frequently. We confiscated all unauthorized stuff from the prisoners, burning a huge pile outside the jail so that the bonfire would send a strong message to rogue elements. As another step, I ordered strict compliance of the jail manual which soon landed me in trouble when two MLAs from the Opposition came to the jail to meet some prisoners without following the jail procedure. Since they had come in their private capacity, I refused to let them enter. Hell broke loose and they filed a privilege motion against me in the Assembly. The state government stood with me but the Speaker had to find a way out or I would have been punished by the Assembly. He asked me to apologize to the MLAs, which I refused to do. In an effort to smoothen matters, the Speaker said that he would tell the MLAs that I had apologized to him and the matter should be closed. I objected to this, saying I would not apologize to anyone as I had done no wrong. Not giving up, he said that he would tell them whatever he wanted to say and I shouldn't have a problem with that. Obviously, I had nothing to say, and thus the matter got sorted out.

After feeling reassured that the security measures were tighter, I made the state government get some top leaders of the insurgents, including N. Bisheshwar Singh, founder of the PLA, back from Naini Jail in Allahabad to the Imphal jail, assuring the Chief Minister that we would ensure that he and the others could not escape. My junior officer, Karanjit Singh, told me that he would stay in the same cell of the jail with Bisheshwar Singh! The leaders were brought to the Imphal jail and from the very beginning, we were tough with them. To hit back, they started complaining to the court that I was trying to poison them. We later became a trifle friendly with them and I brought Bisheshwar to the negotiation table to have a discussion with the Chief Minister. Some other talks were also held, but unfortunately nothing came out of this.

Later, I wrote a novel, *Rebels of the Valley*, published in 1987, on the insurgency in Manipur. I had predicted in the book then—based on my assessment of the situation—that the insurgency would continue there in the future as well. It has turned out to be true as even today, after four decades, the separatist groups continue their armed conflict with the security forces.

A little later, I was posted as the Home Secretary of the state, a rare thing for an IPS officer, with the additional charge of IG (Prisons). It was a great learning experience and a better support to the security forces fighting the insurgency there. I think that Home Departments of the states and the Centre should have more police officers as dealing with internal security is a professional job and such officers with their knowledge and experience will be more useful. Once, there was a lot of pressure on me to release some of the top insurgents on parole, but I didn't give in. I wrote the reasons for my opposition on the file for the Chief Minister to read, but it came back from him without any comment. On another occasion, the Chief Minister wanted me to recruit some boys from his community in the police, but since they were too short to meet the height requirements, I could not oblige and sent a note to him, giving the reasons. He was upset with me but he neither said anything nor did he write anything on that note.

I was also in charge of the Rehabilitation Department and was instrumental in opening a rehabilitation centre, Gandhi Peace Camp, for surrendered insurgents. My book, *The Thorns*, based on the prevailing criminal justice system, was also published during this time. When I presented a copy to S.M.H. Burney, the then Governor of Manipur, he remarked that as Home Secretary at the Centre, he never had the time to write a book. It was difficult to gauge whether it was a dig or a compliment, but I took it as a compliment!

Now let us turn to an interesting episode depicting the culture of that beautiful part of India. While I was the Home Secretary, H. Jelshyam (a Kuki tribal and IAS officer of the 1966 batch who was the Commissioner of Works) walked into my office along with another person. After greeting me, they both sat down. He told me that I had to help the person with him in sorting out some issue as he was his brother and a peon in my office! I was dumbstruck. When he saw my reaction, he said, 'You bloody north Indians forget your brothers and sisters when in high positions but here we do not. For your information, my brother and I live together with our families in my bungalow and have a common kitchen. We both come together to office where he does his work and I do mine. Any objection?' Of course, I had no answer.

Close kinship is prevalent there. The women have a high status in society and in one market, called Ima Market (*ima* means mother) in Imphal, only women can be shopkeepers. Women have been in the forefront of social movements, and the patriarchal system is not followed. They also have a choice when it comes to marriage. Most of the marriages among Meiteis are by elopement, a tradition following the legend in the *Mahabharata* that Arjuna, the Pandava famous for his archery, had married the warrior princess, Chitraganda, after eloping with her. Formal divorces are rare in Manipur and women have the freedom to marry or leave anyone. There is no stigma in being a single mother. Their clothing and food are also unique. The women wear the *phanek*, which is a sarong or wraparound skirt. In weddings, the bride is dressed like Radha, the consort of Lord Krishna, the dress in which the *Ras Lila* is also performed by the locals. 'Manipuri' is a very famous classical dance and the people excel in playing musical instruments and martial arts.

Fish is a major part of the Manipuri diet. The cooks maintain a high level of hygiene while cooking Manipuri food formally, making sure that they bathe before cooking. They keep the kitchen clean and cover their noses with a piece of cloth to avoid spreading germs. In formal functions, the locals eat in a squatting position and are served a full meal on banana leaves, resulting in wastage at times. Among the festivals, Thabal Chongba (a folk dance performed in the moonlight during Holi to the sound of cymbals, drums and flutes) is very vibrant. In different *leikai*s, boys and girls pick up their love partners for the dance. On the day of Holi in Imphal, various groups wearing pure white clothes move from their homes to the Govindaji Temple where the priest sprinkles pink-coloured water on their clothes.

Politically, the Congress was the ruling party followed by the Manipur People's Party. However, like elsewhere in India, politicians here often crossed over or defected to the other party. Development in the state was also insignificant. For example, the telephone system was inefficient. Those were the days of trunk calls to other cities. Once when my family was there, I sent my two elder daughters to Delhi by air and it took us almost 24 hours to know whether they had reached Delhi safely. My wife and I had to sit in the telephone exchange for many hours to make this important call.

Overall, in addition to serious work, I also enjoyed my stay there. We attended many parties which the officers in the army as well as other forces organized regularly, although these were small gatherings as the officers were few in number. It was a great learning experience to work in an insurgency-infested state where police functioning is totally different. And it was a great exposure to a new land with a rich history, geography and culture, a colourful part of India.

After completing close to three years, I started looking for a deputation to Delhi, although it was difficult. In those days, I had a chance meeting with Atal Bihari Vajpayee, later the Prime Minister of India. I was travelling from Delhi to Imphal on a flight with various stops on the way. At Delhi, by chance I got a seat next to Vajpayee and Bhairon Singh Shekhawat, another well-known BJP leader, who later became the Vice-President of India. They were going to Guwahati. I mentioned to Vajpayee that I wanted to leave Imphal and would like to work with him, as I was also politically inclined. He said that I was welcome, but on hearing that my only source of income was my job, he told me that the party would not be able to pay me a sufficient amount so I should weigh the pros and cons before joining. He also said that in politics one can never be certain about the future.

When we landed at Bagdogra (in Darjeeling district of West Bengal) for a stopover, I took both of them for a cup of tea and snacks to the restaurant in the lounge. Later, I decided to forget about joining him though, at times, I regret not grabbing the chance as my life would have taken a different turn.

Many years later when Bhairon Singh Shekhawat was the Vice-President of India, someone I knew who was close to him, took me along to meet him though I wasn't that keen. He told me on the way that Shekhawat had a photographic memory. I tried to test this and during our meeting with him, I casually mentioned that I had met him once in the aircraft when he was going to Guwahati along with Vajpayee. Indeed, he remembered it and recalled that I had taken them for tea to the restaurant at Bagdogra and had also ordered *pakora*s (crispy vegetable fritters) for them! When it was time to leave, I stood up and saluted him.

During a flight in 2000, I was allotted seat next to the Rashtriya Swayamsevak Sangh (RSS) chief K.S. Sudarshan. During our conversation, he told me that China was a bigger threat to India and he was not worried about Pakistan. Similarly, once I had former Home Minister Sushil Kumar Shinde as my companion in the aircraft.

Reverting to my search for a deputation to Delhi from Manipur, the DG of the CRPF, who had come to Imphal, offered me a posting in Punjab when I requested him to take me on deputation. However, I wanted Delhi and politely declined his offer. Eventually, I got selected in the Central Bureau of Investigation (CBI) in Delhi after all my efforts. I left Manipur a little better on the insurgency front with satisfaction of having done my bit. Landing in Delhi in March 1984, I couldn't join because some officers, who had joined as DSPs in the CBI, wanted their promotion first and got a stay order from the Supreme Court against any induction of IPS officers as DIGs in the CBI till they got their promotion.

I engaged Soli Sorabjee, the famous lawyer, to plead on my behalf in the court and to state that I may be allowed to join without prejudice to their interest as some posts of DIG could be kept vacant for the petitioners. I paid him Rs 2,200 as fee, a large sum for me. The court rejected my request. There was some rumour that the petitioners had some influence among one of the judges, which was why this judgement was passed. It meant that I was without a job and pay for almost nine months.

A shameful occurrence in India's history during that time was the atrocities against the Sikhs, mostly in Delhi and some other parts of India, subsequent to the assassination of Indira Gandhi on 31 October 1984 in New Delhi. Her decision to launch Operation Blue Star in June 1984 to flush out terrorists hiding in the Golden Temple, the pre-eminent spiritual shrine of Sikhism, boomeranged, leading to anger among the Sikhs and impelling two Sikh bodyguards to shoot her dead at her residence. After her cremation, I visited the site of her funeral pyre and saw that no police and security forces were around. Such is the fate of the most powerful people on earth.

The assassination sparked tremendous anger against the Sikhs, who were viciously attacked in Delhi and other places. Thousands lost their lives and at many places, mobs were led by or instigated by some leaders of the Congress Party, which was in power. Rajiv Gandhi, the son of Indira Gandhi, had taken over as Prime Minister and he unfortunately justified this pogrom later by saying that when a big tree gets uprooted, there are bound to be repercussions. The Delhi Police didn't or couldn't handle the situation and the army was not called in soon enough. In the Karol Bagh area of Delhi, I saw a Sikh man being dragged on the road and a truck tyre being put on fire to garland the hapless man with it. I was alone in my personal car at that time and couldn't do anything to stop this inhuman act. In our house in Bharat Nagar, we had to bring quite a few Sikh families of our colony to stay with us. We had to ferry many Sikh friends and families to places of safety from their homes, from various locations, including railway stations, when they reached Delhi from some other place. This genocide, as some call it, will remain a blot on India's history. No timely action was taken against the criminals or balm applied to the sufferers.

Rajiv Gandhi called for general elections and riding on a sympathy wave, the Congress won a huge majority in Parliament. The BJP got just two seats, one each from Andhra and Gujarat. None of the tall leaders, including Vajpayee, got elected.

Reverting to my story, I was suddenly asked to join the CRPF one afternoon. It so happened that I had gone to meet V.K. Jain, Joint Secretary in charge of the police in the Home Ministry, to inquire about any development with regard to my posting. In those days, cadre officers of the CRPF, BSF and other forces were on a spree getting stay orders against the induction of IPS officers in their forces. Jain was an excellent officer and a very helpful person. He told me to meet the DG CRPF right then and report for duty as some CRPF officers were also likely to get a stay order from some court against the induction of IPS officers in the force. I was not even dressed for a formal meeting with the DG but I rushed to the CRPF headquarters in Lodi Colony. The DG told me that I would be posted to Chandigarh and I should move there the next day. Having said a 'No' to this posting in Punjab earlier to him, I accepted my fate—I was destined to join the CRPF and in Punjab. Had I known that ultimately this would happen to me, I would have joined there nine months ago, rather than going through the harassment of court procedures and being without a job and pay for such a long period. But we all have to bow to destiny and that is what happened. As it turned out, the posting was beneficial for me, both personally and professionally. I believe that whatever God does for us is always for the best though we realize this only later on.

Chapter 8

Punjab and the Capital

During the last week of a cold December in 1984, I landed in Chandigarh to take over as DIG (Operations) of the CRPF. The state was in the grip of a serious insurgency, and more so after the execution of Operation Blue Star some months earlier during which the army had entered the Golden Temple to capture the Sikh militants who had occupied the holy shrine and were gathering arms and ammunition. This military action led to an uproar against the government. The state was in a turmoil. Pakistan fully exploited the situation by abetting and supporting a few Sikh militant outfits that were creating havoc in the state, demanding Khalistan as a country separate from India. Politics was responsible to quite an extent for this situation in the state. About 40 battalions of the CRPF were deployed all over Punjab to assist the state police in controlling the insurgency. And I happened to be the sole boss of such a large force.

Incidentally, the CRPF was initially raised as the Crown Representative Police in 1939 at Neemuch in Madhya Pradesh as a force to assist the then British government to suppress rebellions and maintain law and order. After Independence, it was rechristened as the Central Reserve Police Force through the enactment of the CRPF Act, 1949 by Parliament. It is the largest active paramilitary force in the world with a sanctioned strength of more than three lakh personnel in 246 battalions (as in 2019) including some Mahila Battalions. CRPF personnel are sent to the aid of state police forces in maintaining law and order, handling communal riots, tackling Maoists in Chhattisgarh and Jharkhand, insurgents in the North-East, terrorists in Jammu and Kashmir as well as beefing up VIP security. The CRPF has specialized units like the Rapid Action Force deployed in communally sensitive areas and the Commando Battalions for Resolute Action (CoBRA) deployed mostly in Naxalite-affected areas. Its role has expanded over the years and its growth as a formidable force has also been phenomenal. Most of its personnel are always on the move, which is why they are fondly called '*Chalte Raho Pyare Fauj*' in a lighter vein.

It was a great management and operational challenge for me in Punjab. On the very first day, one of my staff officers brought me a list of about three dozen officers from different battalions for 'ops' (operational) clearance for leaving the state on duty elsewhere or for going on leave. I told him that it was up to the COs to relieve them or not, depending on the unit's operational responsibilities. He told me that the orders from the CRPF headquarters stipulated that my permission would be required. I told him to ignore those orders, gave 'ops' clearance for these officers and asked him to issue orders restoring the authority of the COs in this matter. I felt that this would lead to more efficiency as officers would not be on tenterhooks before they could go on leave and feel the need to make frantic calls to my staff officer for early clearance. He warned me that our headquarters would not like their orders to be to disobeyed. I told him not to worry and that I would deal with it. This order diminished his importance for obvious reasons, which is why he wasn't happy about it. The COs welcomed this order but I did get into a tiff with the very senior DIG

(Operations) at the headquarters who took exception to this act. I reported the matter to the DG who sided with me, but my relations with that senior officer got ruptured. Such things do happen in service.

I had started my tenure with a visit to the Golden Temple in Amritsar to offer prayers, as instructed by my mother. After that I toured a lot and visited each and every CRPF post. N.N. Vohra IAS was the Home Secretary of Punjab (he later became the Governor of J&K) and K.P.S. Gill was the DGP for some period during my tenure, both highly competent officers, who gave full support to the CRPF. There were many day-to-day problems on many fronts, but the CRPF acquitted itself well with its highly experienced commandants and other senior officers as well as support from the local authorities. K.P.S. Gill is credited with ending insurgency in Punjab. I had worked with the renowned police officer in different capacities in service and was in touch with him all through his life. It is a matter of regret that he didn't get enough formal recognition for his service to the nation so richly deserved by him.

One major problem was the presence of a number of COs in one district, which, naturally, had one district SP from the state government who had put in less years of service than the COs. They expected the SP to be very respectful to each one of them, but the SP obviously had no time or any inclination to cater to their egos, which led to problems. Another big challenge was to keep the morale of the force high, especially of the lower ranks. I used to have regular meetings with the jawans in a format called a *Durbar* or *Sainik Sammelan*. The idea always was to exhort them to do their job well, to listen to their difficulties and sort these out to the extent possible. In one such meeting in Jalandhar, which was attended by more than 500 personnel of different ranks, one of the jawans stood up and pleaded for a CRPF Public School to be opened, with hostel facilities on the pattern of such schools set up by the defence forces, the BSF and other forces. His reason was that the family system in the villages had broken down and they were unable to look after their families due to the regular movement of this force. I appreciated his point but told him that such matters take time. I also told him that I would forward his suggestion to the CRPF headquarters. However, this important requirement got stuck in my mind. Later in the CRPF when I became DIG (Administration), I made a concerted effort and with the help of many supporters was able to open first such school in Rohini in Delhi with hostel facilities. I had the blessings of then DG S.D. Pandey and IG (Headquarters) B.J.S. Sial, but more of that later.

During my tenure in Punjab, I had been allotted a government flat in Chandigarh where my family would visit occasionally. When J.F. Ribeiro took over as the DG CRPF and came to visit Punjab, I accompanied him on his first trip, which was to Amritsar. In the evening, when we were sipping a drink at the Mess of a battalion prior to the formal dinner in honour of the visiting DG, I got a call from my staff officer from Chandigarh. He told me not to worry, but that he had been informed that two terrorists were looking for my address in Chandigarh. They had been tipped off by a guard of the Punjab Police at the residence of a VIP. Immediately, my staff officer had rushed to my house and finding that my wife had gone to the market nearby, followed her there and brought her back home. He placed the required guards there and made other security arrangements.

Ribeiro asked me about the call because I must have looked perturbed, so I told him what I had heard. He shrugged his shoulders and said, 'It's part of the profession.' I agreed and told him that I had faced similar situations in Manipur also when I occasionally got threats and exactly the same thing had happened—my wife was brought back from the market in Imphal after some information about insurgents looking for my family.

The situation in Punjab continued to be turbulent for some more years before it was sorted out. Terrorism in the state was created by politics and was finally curbed by the political will shown by Chief Minister Beant Singh. He, however, had to pay the price for it later—he was killed in a suicide bombing outside the Punjab Civil Secretariat on 31 August 1995. The Khalistan separatist group, Babbar Khalsa, claimed responsibility for the assassination.

Anyway, the CRPF was acquitting itself very well in operations against terrorists and maintaining peace to the extent possible, strongly supporting the local police.

Meanwhile, I got transferred to Delhi as DIG Range, CRPF, in the latter part of 1985. This was a different kind of job, more of an administrative assignment rather than an operational one, but it also posed many challenges. The battalions of my range were deployed in other areas of India and vice versa. I had operational control over them, but no official administrative control as per rules which led to its own difficulties. I decided to ignore this impediment and tried to ensure that the units in Delhi were also administratively comfortable. There were about a dozen battalions in Delhi, mostly guarding the residences of VIPs and government offices. The headquarters of these units were in makeshift arrangements, giving the impression that they were temporary residents, which was not the case. Additionally, they had to receive or see off the battalions going to Punjab and returning from there, and make transitory accommodation and food available for them. There were many other problems that needed to be tackled on priority. To assist me, I had picked Ramesh Chandra, a young, smart and competent Deputy CO as my staff officer. I had first met him in Faridkot in Punjab and was impressed with him. He was indeed a big help in my tenure here.

In one of the early meetings of the COs, I raised the issue of adequate space for the units and told them that we needed to do something on this score. One of the COs, K. Kesavan of the 10th Battalion located in the Delhi Police Lines in Kingsway Camp, told me bluntly that many senior officers like me had talked of the same issue in the past but nothing had been done. I got a bit irritated but held myself back. I thought that indeed it was for me to prove that we could succeed. I have earlier mentioned about my meeting with Union Minister for Information and Broadcasting H.K.L. Bhagat on this land issue. We had posted a guard at his residence, which was our connection with him. With Bhagat's help, the Vice-Chairman of the DDA gave us one plot of land in Okhla area on the very same day. It was a pleasant surprise. Getting land in Delhi at once was like buying an item off the shelf! He solved the mystery by saying that they had demolished an unauthorized colony on DDA land that day itself and he was afraid that the encroachers would come back to settle there again, as often happened in Delhi. By different ways and means, he gave us about six to seven plots.

Commandant Kesavan later apologized for his rude remarks in our earlier meeting on the land issue and appreciated my efforts. But the land issue still remained, as we needed accommodation for a significant number of incoming and outgoing battalions from and to Punjab via Delhi. All these battalions were forced to share space with the existing units in Delhi who found it extremely difficult to accommodate this huge additional manpower in addition to their own personnel at their locations on a regular basis. We badly needed transit accommodation for this purpose.

An opportunity came when Arun Nehru was appointed as the Minister of State (Home) by Prime Minister Rajiv Gandhi. Both were close friends, so Arun Nehru was very powerful. One day, the DG CRPF, S.D. Pandey, was asked to brief him about the force. That morning I went to the North Block to the office of the DG on my own and sent a note to my new IG (Northern Sector) (called Sector III at that time), K.L. Watts, who was inside the room of the DG where they were discussing plans to brief the minister. Watts, who was a very formal gentleman, came out in a rather bad mood and asked me what I was doing there. I told him that since he and the DG were going to brief the minister, I wanted him to request the minister to direct the Lieutenant Governor of Delhi to give us a piece of land in Delhi for the CRPF. Luckily, the IG agreed and took me inside to meet the DG. When I told the DG what the purpose of my unscheduled visit was, he agreed that the request should be made. The idea worked and Lieutenant Governor H.L. Kapur, a former Vice Air Marshal of the Indian Air Force, asked for a meeting with us at 11 a.m. the same day. Three of us, the DG, IG and I, trooped to his office in old Delhi. We were ushered in as soon as we reached, but there were many people in his office room, so we moved towards the sofa in a corner to wait till his ongoing meeting was over. To our utter surprise, he asked us to join the meeting and told us that the officers present were from departments concerned and had been called to decide about the land to be allotted to the CRPF! We didn't expect that fast an action.

During the discussion, it transpired that the Delhi Police had about 400 acres of land allotted at Wazirabad on the Yamuna riverbed. I told the Lieutenant Governor that an area of 30 acres should be sufficient for us for transit accommodation of battalions going to and coming from Punjab. At once, the Lieutenant Governor ordered 60 acres to be given to us out of those 400 acres. There were muted protests from the DDA and Delhi Police officers present but the LG would have none of it and stuck to his decision, asking me to take over the land that afternoon itself! We did the needful after carrying out the demarcation with Delhi Police officers the same afternoon and put up a transit camp there with temporary accommodation, toilets, kitchens, transport, wireless set-up and other essentials in due course. It was a huge relief for everyone in the CRPF.

On the other pieces of land allotted to us, we built semi-permanent

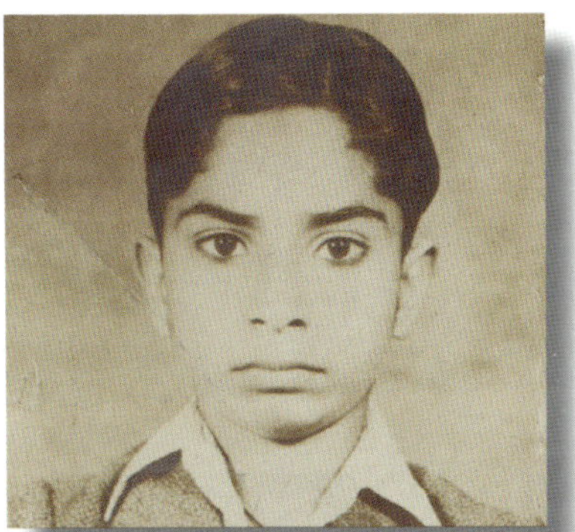

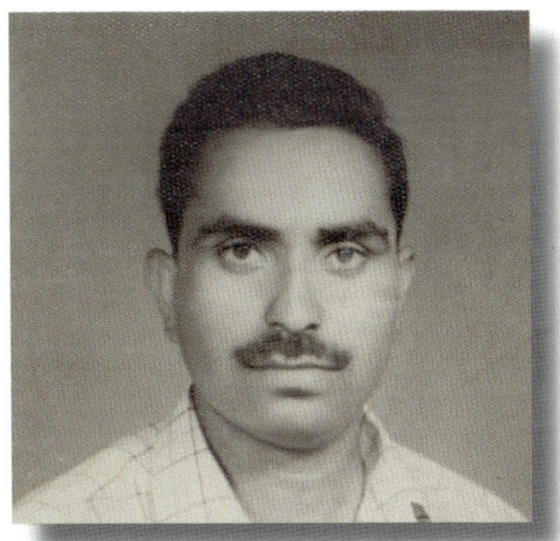

The author as a child (left above), a young man (left below) and an IPS officer

The author (left) enacting the role of Rajguru in the drama *Shahid Bhagat Singh* when he was in Class XI

From left: The author playing the harmonium with close friends M.M.K. Katial (on the flute), Avinash Makani (also on the flute) and Balbir Singh (on the tabla) in 1965. All of them then worked at the Railway Board. Except for Katial, the other three are fake musicians!

The author's parents Shiv Ram Vohra and Sheela Wanti Vohra in Mussoorie

At the National Police Academy, Mount Abu, in October 1968 along with Inspector Joseph and Riding Master Janak Singh (both seated in the middle). The author is standing second from left, and Ustad Head Constable Vasudev Singh is in the middle

The author practising shot put during his training at Mount Abu

The author and his wife Chander Mohini Khanna (her name was later changed to Jyoti) during their marriage on 7 May 1970

The couple enjoying a boat ride in Nainital Lake during their honeymoon

The author with his parents, wife Jyoti and eldest daughter Archana at his ancestral house in Bharat Nagar, New Delhi in May 1971

At the farewell organised by the North District of the Delhi Police for DIG R.D. Singh in early 1972. The author is seated third from right and his boss Nikhil Kumar Singh, SP, is seated third from left

After assuming charge as the Superintendant of Police in Agartala in October 1973

With his maternal grandmother Damodari Devi, mother (both seated), wife, daughters and his assistant Constable Birbal, in early 1981

Celebrating 25 years of togetherness on 7 May 1995 with the author's parents-in-law and daughters Archana and Sonya

Inspecting a BSF unit in Jammu, where the author was the Inspector General, in 1998 along with DIG K.S. Vohra and others

The author and his wife visiting the BSF School in Jammu in the latter part of 1998

The author's grandchild Shreya Mehra with his father-in-law Ram Prakash Khanna in 2000. Shreya is the daughter of the author's daughter Archana and son-in-law Rashi

In the hilly terrain of Tripura on 4 November 2001 on the trail of insurgents

Having lunch in a hut during the same patrol mentioned above

With President R. Venkatraman at the Rashtrapati Bhawan during the conference of DGPs in 1991. The author was then DGP Manipur

The author presenting a copy of his book *Manav Adhikar aur Police Bal* to President S.D. Sharma at the Rashtrapati Bhawan in 1995

With President K.R. Narayanan at the Rashtrapati Bhawan during the conference of DGPs in 2000. The author was then DGP Tripura

The author and his wife with former President A.P.J. Abdul Kalam in New Delhi in 2008

With Prime Minister Indira Gandhi after a parade in her honour at Kingsway Camp in the Delhi Police Lines in 1970. The author is standing first from the right along with other Company commanders

The author's daughter Archana presenting a bouquet to Prime Minister Rajiv Gandhi at the passing-out parade of the first Mahila Battalion of CRPF in New Delhi on 7 March 1987. The author, who was then DIG (Range) CRPF, is on the extreme right

The author's wife (extreme left) with Mrs Sonia Gandhi during the passing-out parade of the first Mahila Battalion of CRPF in New Delhi on 7 March 1987

The author, who was then DGP Manipur, greeting Prime Minister Chandra Shekhar Singh at a conference in New Delhi in March 1991

With Prime Minister P.V. Narasimha Rao at the Anniversary Parade of the CISF on 10 March 1994. The author was then IG CISF

With Prime Minister H.D. Deve Gowda at the Anniversary Parade of the CISF on 10 March 1997. The author was then IG CISF

The author with Prime Minister Atal Bihari Vajpayee and Home Minister L.K. Advani during the annual conference of DGPs in 2001

The author presenting a copy of his book, *Tripura's Bravehearts: A Police Success Story of Counterinsurgency*, to Prime Minister Manmohan Singh in 2012

The author with Union Home Minister Giani Zail Singh in 1980 during a conference. Zail Singh became the President of India later on

Union Home Minister Buta Singh pinning the Police Medal for Meritorious Service on the author at the Anniversary Parade of CRPF in 1986

The author with Defence Minister George Fernandes in Agartala in 2002. He was then DGP Tripura

The author, as the IG BSF Jammu, presenting a memento to Jammu & Kashmir Chief Minister Farooq Abdullah during a golf tournament held at the BSF Campus in 1997

The author standing behind (right) Tripura Chief Minister Manik Sarkar during the Independence Day Parade in Agartala on 15 August 2000. He was then DGP Tripura

The author (second from right), who was DIG CRPF Punjab at the time, with Julio Ribeiro, DG CRPF, in Amritsar in June 1985

The author speaking during the release function of his book, *Don't Laugh, We are Police* at the India International Centre, New Delhi on 14 February 1995. Former Home Secretary N.N. Vohra (centre) was the chief guest while former DGP of Punjab K.P.S. Gill released the book

Justice Ranganath Misra, former CJI and first Chairperson of the National Human Rights Commission, releasing the author's book on Human Rights and Police in Hindi (*Manav Adhikar Aur Police Bal*) at India International Centre on 7 March 1995

The author, as IG BSF, getting ready for an aerial reconnaissance of forward areas in Jammu and Kashmir in 1998

A family photo after the author's farewell parade on retirement on 31 March 2004. (From left) N.K. Mehra, the author's daughter Archana's father-in-law, Archana, her husband Rashi, daughter Sonya with her daughter Tia, Jyoti, the author, Anuj, husband of daughter Manika (next to him) and Rajnish, Sonya's husband

Parvathi, wife of the author's dear friend and batchmate S. Ramakrishnan (standing left), presenting a bouquet to Jyoti on their arrival for the farewell parade, organised by Ramakrishnan with affection, on 31 March 2004

With the author's batchmates and their wives after his farewell parade.
Standing from left: S. Ramakrishnan, M.R. Reddy, B.B. Mishra, R.K. Sharma, M.K. Singh, Naginder Singh, the author, Jyoti Sinha and Anil Pande
Seated from left: Mrs Mishra, Mrs Reddy, Mrs Sharma, Jyoti and Parvathi

The author addressing participants during a training workshop on High Impact Presentation Skills for M5 Trainers in 2005

The author and his wife dancing during the Holi celebrations at Gymkhana Club, New Delhi, in 2018

A visit to Santa Claus in Lapland, Finland on 17 June 2015. Rovaniemi in Lapland is the 'official hometown' of Santa Claus

The author and his wife during a wedding in 2018 (left) and at their Imphal home in 1992

Clockwise: The author with his wife Jyoti and daughters Archana, Sonya and Manika at the Taj Mahal, Agra, in February 2022. Jyoti's sister Neelam and her husband Anil Jaggi. Jyoti's brother Satish Khanna. The author's grandchildren: (from left) Shreya, Vansh, Aadit, Avi, Tia and Ayaan accommodation to replace tents, mostly with material provided by the Central Public Works Department (CPWD), an unusual step but managed with a lot of effort, including barracks, other space and transit accommodation for officers visiting Delhi. In the barracks, starting with Andheria Mor in Delhi, we installed bunk charpoys for the jawans as the men outnumbered the number of available single charpoys that could be accommodated. Water for drinking and other uses was also arranged with help from the authorities concerned.

This effort was followed up by putting up prefabricated huts for the security guards at various locations, which replaced tents and made life comfortable for jawans in different climatic conditions in Delhi. These huts were also set up for a central Transit Officers' Mess (TOM became popular word for it) in a battalion at Rabindra Rangshala on the ridge between Karol Bagh and Dhaula Kuan in Delhi. Initially, locating and setting these up was a huge exercise. After trying to contact many manufacturers, but failing, I persuaded my then IG, Shivmohan Singh, to advertise in the newspapers, asking manufacturers of prefabricated huts to put up their samples in a battalion on a certain date. There was an overwhelming response and about more than a dozen firms set up samples, out of which one was selected and orders placed after due formalities. This was quite an achievement and gave relief to the jawans. We started with the replacement of tents of guards in the embassies of the Chanakyapuri area on Shanti Path of New Delhi. The rest as they say is history. We went on a spree and other forces also started following the trend.

Talking of transit camps, I also opened one such camp at the Old Delhi Railway Station for jawans and others travelling by trains to help them with their stay, reservations and other coordination regarding transport.

In Chandigarh also, my IG, Shivmohan Singh, and I met the then Haryana Chief Minister Bhajan Lal and persuaded him to give us a big piece of land in Panchkula for a Group Centre of the CRPF. Punjab and Haryana were then a part of the jurisdiction of my IG (Sector III) (later renamed as Northern Sector). I learnt a lot from IG Shivmohan Singh personally and professionally, especially his public relations skills. The way he talked to the Chief Minister was so persuasive that the land was promised at once. The IG had told him the proposed Group Centre would benefit Haryana because it would lead to the employment of hundreds of youth from the state, apart from the employment of labour for the construction of buildings there. Now, at 95 years, his faculties are intact and occasionally we talk to each other.

However, there were many other small issues to be dealt with. On the operational front, I recall that a CRPF post was established at the residence of a former Lieutenant Governor who refused to give access to the jawans to the toilet there. The jawans had nowhere else to go to ease themselves. We had to put our foot down till some arrangement was made, so he gave in. Then vouchers for air travel for COs at government cost were always sent by post, leading to delays. So I gave these to them in advance to use only after my approval was conveyed. There were many such problems but we were able to solve most of them.

During this period, two new units also came up which meant that some administrative and operational issues cropped up. One was the Special Duty Group (SDG) to guard the outer perimeter of the residence of the Prime Minister and the second was the raising of the first Mahila Battalion, 88th (M) Battalion of the CRPF. Both had challenges—the first, regarding the selection and training of manpower along with the provision of special weapons and other logistics, and the second, to cater to various special needs of women. Just one example is how we had sanctioned barbers for the unit, but had to make special recruitments and buy different items that are used for women, simultaneously rechristening the barber shop as a parlour! M.P. Chitnis as the CO of the SDG unit and S.A. Khan as the CO of the Mahila Battalion did a fantastic job. Certain standards were set by the first Mahila Battalion on various issues, which became a benchmark for the Mahila Battalions that came up later.

The POP of this first Mahila Battalion took place on 7 March 1987 when I was DIG Range, CRPF, New Delhi. Rajiv Gandhi, the then Prime Minister, had come to the Group Centre of the CRPF in Jharoda Kalan to take the salute. On that occasion, it was my daughter Archana who presented him with a bouquet on his arrival at the venue.

Later, during the Prime Minister's interaction with the officers, I told him that CRPF COs did not even have the power to sanction a telephone for units in the new locations where they are deployed, and had to depend on the state governments even for this minor necessity. He was shocked and looked at Arun Nehru, the then Minister of State (Internal Security), who smartly said that the necessary orders would be issued. However, these orders never saw the light of day even though the matter was later taken up officially with the Ministry of Home Affairs, quoting the orders of the Prime Minister. I was also a witness to another such incident. In 1989, the then Prime Minister V.P. Singh came to take the salute during the Golden Jubilee parade of the CRPF. I was the Deputy Director (DD) (Administration) then. At our request, he announced the sanction of a Golden Jubilee Medal for CRPF personnel during his speech at the parade, but that also never came. So powerful is the bureaucracy in India that it can defy even the orders of the Prime Minister!

Due to some jurisdictional issues, I was also in charge of Gujarat with regard to the deployment of the CRPF even though I could have been given additional charge of Rajasthan bordering Delhi, if required. As often happens in huge organizations, certain arrangements in the CRPF were started because they were required at a certain time, but continued to be in place even when there was no longer any need for them. This jurisdiction of mine was one such example. My job also included extensive touring to inspect my administrative battalions deployed outside Delhi besides attending to many official duties assigned by the higher authorities. This force made me almost do a Bharat Darshan!

During this tenure, I was awarded the Indian Police Medal for Meritorious Service which was pinned on my chest in the anniversary parade of the CRPF by Buta Singh, the then Union Home Minister. And to add to the joy in the family, a photograph of the moment when the medal was pinned was prominently placed on the front page of the *Hindustan Times* the very next day. This was one of the many medals that I was awarded in service.

On the family front, I was allotted a flat in Nanak Pura in Moti Bagh area, not far from my office in R.K. Puram, and we made ourselves comfortable there. Playing tennis regularly every morning in the compound of the 62nd Battalion in the Ridge area (the battalion was led by Y.N. Kashyap) became a feature of life apart from meetings, parties, official functions and parades. Life was on a roll. Of course, we didn't have an air conditioner so installed a cooler instead. There was no geyser in the bathroom for heating water in winter; instead, we had to use an iron rod or a boiler for this purpose every year. I just couldn't afford these luxuries but we didn't feel that we were missing much. Today, even junior officers have these facilities because pay packets have improved. During our stay in Nanak Pura, we travelled to Singapore to visit a friend in 1986. It was great to see how its leaders, mainly first Prime Minister Lee Kuan Yew, had transformed Singapore from a fishing village to an excellent modern state. Yew's autobiography is worth reading.

After about two years, again it was transfer time and I got shifted to the Force Headquarters as the DD (Administration), for a different job, with new challenges. I was deskbound from morning till late in the evening every day with no respite. Moreover, I had many visiting bosses and colleagues in the same building, the pressure on me eventually leading to health issues. Apart from the routine of handling a few hundred files every day, there were meetings too. I used to reach office very early and go home quite late. Even on Sundays and other holidays, I had to work. So much so that I fell sick and suffered from health problems including ulcers in the stomach. Looking after my health became a priority and one of the solutions, apart from medication, was to reorganize my routine. For ulcers, I was advised to have lunch at a fixed time no matter what, but this was not happening due to visitors and frequent summons from seniors. Then I fixed 1 p.m. as my lunch time on the advice of a friend and anybody sitting with me would be requested to join me for lunch. Some people got the message and decided not to enter my room from 1 to 1.30 p.m.

One day, my DG called me soon after 1 p.m. As I was having lunch, I sent word that I would meet him as soon as my lunch was over. I was afraid that this message wouldn't go down well with him, so I finished my lunch quickly and rushed to his room to apologize for not appearing at once. But he was very understanding and told me that he would take care not to disturb me during that half an hour in future. It was a big relief. I'm following that timing till date, except in exceptional circumstances. I now believe that regularity in timings of meals plays a big part in keeping anyone in good health.

To reduce the pressure of going through so many files, I analyzed the situation over a week and reached the conclusion that many of the files need not come to me and could be delegated to juniors. Actually, some files had started coming to the table of DD (Administration) when the size of the force, and hence that of the headquarters, was small. For example, files relating to sanctioning casual leave for constable rank orderlies working in the headquarters, which could be easily handled by the department concerned, were also being sent to me. It surprised me that by this exercise I was able to reduce the number of files I had to see to about two dozen a day from about 200 or so! With the help of my efficient staff, we managed to do quite a few useful things.

Apart from opening the CRPF Public School, along with hostel facilities in Rohini area in Delhi in 1987, I visited some of the best schools around the country to learn about best practices. The institution was first housed in tents on about 10 acres of land allotted by the Ministry of Urban Affairs. Some ground work had already been done by my predecessor and the land had been earmarked by the concerned government agency. The school principal was selected out of more than a hundred applicants with the help of an expert, and the teachers were also given their jobs after strict vetting. We gave them the Central government pay scales. It was decided that none of the relatives of any CRPF personnel would be employed as teachers or staff members. Similarly, the selection of architects for the school building was also done with the help of an expert and eventually, a government department, the National Building Construction Corporation (NBCC), was selected for construction. All such steps were carefully taken, resulting in it becoming one of the finest schools.

For funding, apart from the Education Fund, we requested each employee to contribute one rupee only every month, which built up to a sufficient sum. But I faced a problem. Some of my jealous colleagues complained to the IB and CBI, stating that I had misappropriated funds meant for the school—they pursued this so forcefully that a senior IB officer came and spoke to me about it! But these things often happen in service. The school got such a fine reputation that in the third year of its becoming operational we got a recommendation from the Rashtrapati Bhawan for the admission of a child! All this was possible because of the support given by DG S.D. Pandey, IG (Headquarters) B.J.S. Sial, CO SDG M.P. Chitnis, and efficient

Deputy COs, Gurcharan Singh, G. Kuppuswamy and R.K. Dua. Commandant Kesavan was also a big help.

We also opened an Industrial Training Institute (ITI) for the children of CRPF personnel at Wazirabad in Delhi with the full support of P.S. Bhinder, the Additional DG (he was the Commissioner of Police of Delhi earlier) who had joined by then.

Later, the CRPF opened more schools on this pattern. It has been a big relief to CRPF personnel and a big satisfaction for me as generations of children of CRPF personnel and others have studied and will continue to study there. Many of them have excelled in life.

A Commendation Disc from the DG to the deserving personnel was also introduced, which is another lasting contribution to all the Central armed police forces (earlier called paramilitary forces) and other police forces of the country. I would like to narrate in brief the story behind it. At the headquarters, the DD (Communications) was Brigadier (Retd) Joginder Singh, who always had the Commendation Disc awarded to him by the Army Chief pinned on his uniform. I had noticed it many times but couldn't make out what it was. One day I asked him and he explained to me. I thought of introducing it in the CRPF because the number of Indian Police Medals for Meritorious Service awarded to the CRPF personnel each year was too few compared to our recommendations. This was due to the quotas fixed by the Ministry of Home Affairs for various Central police forces.

On my request, Brig. Joginder Singh got me a copy of the orders about the Commendation Disc from the Army Headquarters, and I sent a proposal on those lines with required modifications to the DG. In the system, the approval of the Home Ministry was required for introducing something new like this, but the ministry was generally touchy about any additional financial expenditure. In this case, I had found out that each disc would cost a couple of rupees so we needed no money from the government for this. The matter was first discussed with the officers concerned and the proposal sent. After that, the concerned Joint Secretary rang me up to say that we could approve of this disc being awarded to deserving officers of all the Central police forces. I agreed at once and the die was cast. Later the disc was copied by almost all the state police forces. It has been a huge morale booster for officers and men as recognition of good work is always important. As the DGP, Tripura from 2000 to 2002, when the state was facing a serious insurgency, I introduced it there, and this initiative played an important role in containing the situation. During that tenure, the CRPF also celebrated its Golden Jubilee in a befitting manner with various functions and a CRPF postage stamp was released.

Some other steps were also taken in the administration branch. All welfare schemes were streamlined and a few more introduced. The number of scholarships for the wards of the CRPF personnel was increased and a rehabilitation cell for retired and disabled personnel was opened. In addition, the designation of the Sector IG was changed from the IG (Sector III), for example, to the IG (Northern Sector), and the Additional DIGs of Group Centres were asked to go on tours to their battalions located in other states on operational duties. To coordinate the supply of provisioning items, the annual administration report of the force for the ministry was written at the headquarters by me rather than getting individual reports from field formations, saving lakhs of papers and the hard work by the field staff through proper channels starting from the battalions.

Jyoti and I are very fond of travelling and visiting different places. In 1989, we visited friends in Hong Kong, Japan and the USA. During our first visit to Hong Kong, we stayed with P.L. Suri, my dear friend who was working with a bank and had moved there from Delhi. Later, Archana and Sonya also visited him and he looked after them and showed them around. They also visited Singapore during that trip. Suri later shifted to London where he lives now.

On our visit to Japan later, we were looked after by Hardev Singh, who is like a younger brother and had lived in Bharat Nagar too. He was dealing with Japanese tourists coming to India and was doing very well. He often graciously said that I was his inspiration to succeed in his life. He accompanied us from Delhi and we stayed with him in his house in Tokyo. He took us around to Mount Fuji and other places. He also took us on a visit to a Japanese family where we witnessed their famous tea ceremony. Japan was a very costly place and continues to be so. We couldn't believe that just two onions cost us about Rs 500 at that time. We also visited Osaka and later Kyoto, where we stayed with a Japanese family, who introduced us to Japanese culture. They made Jyoti wear their traditional dress, the kimono and she, in turn, showed them how a sari is draped.

From Japan we went to Los Angeles in the USA and stayed with Vishal, the son of P.L. Suri, who was studying there. At that time the total cost of one return ticket from New Delhi for this journey was about Rs 18,000. During that trip we also visited Washington, New York, the Niagara Falls and Toronto.

Six years after finishing my satisfying tenure in the CRPF, it was time to go back to Manipur. I had learnt a lot from the CRPF and contributed quite a bit too. The CRPF also looked after us very well. My family remained in Delhi because the children were still studying and an officer posted to the North-East was allowed to retain accommodation in Delhi. We bought the new Maruti Suzuki car which had recently been launched in India and was a big craze. Archana, my eldest daughter, joined Hindu College in Delhi University for Economics (Honours), while Sonya was still in school. Manika, the youngest, had also joined Presentation Convent School near the Red Fort.

Chapter 9

Working in Different Organizations

Back in Manipur, I had to wait for a few days before my orders were issued. I was due to become the IGP in the state. A Manipuri officer, W. Damodar Singh from whom I had taken over as the DIG (Range) during my earlier tenure, was also due for promotion as an IGP. A few days later, he walked into my room at the police headquarters. Full of humour, as he always was, he saluted me, stood at attention and said, 'Sir, since you are more intelligent than me, you have been posted as IG (Intelligence)!'

He became the IGP (Law and Order), which is considered an important field job. Locals are generally preferred on important jobs by the state governments and Manipur was no exception. Again, I was the first in my batch to be promoted as an IG. As it happened, every time I went to Manipur I got a promotion—as a DIG, IG and Director General of Police (DGP)—and always the first in the batch. I was never an Additional IG or Additional DGP.

Nathoo Lal IPS from the UP cadre was the DGP. He was earlier my senior colleague and later my boss in the BPR&D. His tenure was coming to an end. After he left, I was asked to take over as the DGP till a new officer was selected from another state on deputation as the DGP.

During my tenure as the officiating DGP, I introduced the inspection of the Manipur Rifles battalions on the pattern followed by the CRPF, improved and constructed more accommodation for the staff at the police headquarters, upgraded the service conditions of the staff and organized an interaction of senior police officers with the Chief Minister to inform him of the achievements and problems of the police and other matters. One major issue was the financial powers of the police. When a new TV for my office room was purchased, I had to sign about 20 bills for various parts of the TV as my financial powers were too low! The government was responsive to my request and increased the financial powers of the DGP.

Another important episode deserves mention. During the warm-up towards the general election due in 1991, Rajiv Gandhi was supposed to arrive in Imphal for campaigning on 19 May 1991. B.V. Wanchoo, the local AD of the Intelligence Bureau (who was later Director, SPG and Governor of Goa), informed me of his programme. In consultation with local Congress leader R.K. Jaichandra Singh, a former Union minister, it was decided that Rajiv Gandhi would alight at the airport in the forenoon, address a public meeting close by and then fly to Orissa (now Odisha) the same day. We made the necessary security arrangements, but there was one problem. The IB wanted us to arrange a bulletproof car for the former Prime Minister. There was only one such car in the state and it was with Chief Minister R.K. Ranbir Singh of the Manipur People's Party, the ruling party in the state at that time. I met him and requested him to lend his bulletproof car for a few hours but he refused. I had to express my helplessness to the IB. As the DGP, Rajiv Gandhi's security was a big worry for me but we had to make foolproof police and security arrangements for his visit and the public meeting, and that we did. We heaved a sigh of relief when he took off after the meeting.

Two days later, on 21 May, late in the evening when I had gone to bed, Wanchoo rang up to say that Rajiv Gandhi has been assassinated in Sriperumbudur in Tamil Nadu by a suicide bombing at about 10 p.m. in which some more people had also been killed. Even though I thanked my stars that he had gone from Imphal safely, I felt sad at such a tragic death. From Imphal, he had first gone to Odisha and then Tamil Nadu. Another twist to this tale was that when a portion of his ashes was to come to Manipur while being sent to other states also, the Chief Minister called me and told me that he would spare his bulletproof car for the ashes to be carried from the airport! I couldn't help thinking that he didn't give it when Rajiv Gandhi was alive. I have nothing more to say on this except, sadly, to point out how small-minded we are at times.

In another incident, the Chief Minister suddenly called me to his office one morning and asked me to suspend the SHO of a police station. He told me that one MLA of his party, who was sitting there, wanted his suspension. I told the Chief Minister that an officer of that rank cannot be suspended without any basis or inquiry. I offered a solution, saying that if a written complaint against the SHO was given to me for his misconduct, I would get it inquired within 24 hours and suspend him if he was found at fault. The Chief Minister would have none of it. Then I asked him to issue written orders for this suspension and I would take action. He got annoyed and told me, 'If you don't suspend the SHO right now, I will suspend you.' Taken aback but keeping cool, I told him, 'Sir, please do that then.' He looked at me with anger but kept quiet. Some other visitors had walked into his room then but I kept on sitting. After some time, when he asked me why I was not going to my office, I told him, 'Sir, give me my suspension order, and I will go home then and not to the office.'

The Chief Minister asked me to go to his ante-room. Soon after I reached there, he came over and told me, 'Mr Vohra, you don't understand. It is my political necessity to ask you to suspend the SHO.'

I told the Chief Minister that it was unjust to suspend anyone without a proper inquiry and it was also unfair on his part to threaten me with a suspension. I was visibly annoyed. Seeing my expression, the Chief Minister mollified me by giving me a cup of tea and asked me not to suspend the SHO. He said that he would handle the MLA and resolve the matter.

As the DGP Manipur, I attended the annual conference of DGPs convened by IB in Delhi and as a part of the programme, called on President R. Venkataraman. It was a pleasure talking to him exclusively for a few minutes about the situation in Manipur and North-East generally. A perfect gentleman, he was very gracious to all of us.

Apart from my professional work, I collected police jokes from all over India and came up with a book *Don't Laugh, We're Police*. It was when I was looking for a publisher for this book, I came in contact with K.P.R. Nair, the owner of Konark Publishers, who agreed to publish the book and did an excellent job. He has become a friend since then and later published my book on Tripura also. My book on jokes was released by N.N. Vohra and K.P.S. Gill at the India International Centre (IIC). A first of its kind, the book was received very well in the press as the news and reviews showed and by the common person in addition to the police fraternity.

The insurgency was still going on in Manipur. Sometimes excesses by the army, including the Assam Rifles, led to frequent problems between them and the police, but at the same time cooperation in operations was evident.

A. V. Liddle, an IPS officer from the Madhya Pradesh cadre, later took over as DGP Manipur. Soon after, an Indian Airlines flight crashed in Manipur, killing all 69 people aboard. Two of my batchmates, B.S. Rathore and D.S. Amist on deputation to the airlines in vigilance and security jobs, landed in Imphal in connection with this incident and stayed with me. I was also witness to an unpleasant sight of a post-mortem being conducted on 18 bodies simultaneously then.

I continued working in Manipur until I was posted as the Officer on Special Duty in Manipur Bhawan in Delhi on my request, the reason for this being that some rules had created a problem with the retention of my accommodation in Delhi for my family. It could only be sorted out with my posting to Delhi. I had completed more than two years as the IG (Intelligence) in the state before handing over charge and hurriedly left for Delhi to join my new posting as time on the housing issue was running out. But some people in the higher echelons in the state did not take kindly to my leaving Manipur and I wasn't even allowed to go back officially and bring my luggage. I had to depend upon my junior officials to pack up my household stuff and send the lot by train from Dimapur in Nagaland.

At the time of my departure, nothing much had changed since my earlier tenure there. Today, in the first half of 2022, the state still has separatists who take to armed conflict though the situation is much better. The latest incident was the killing of a Colonel of the Assam Rifles, his wife and five-year old son in an ambush near Manipur's border with Myanmar on 13 November 2021. The People's Liberation Army (PLA), named after the Chinese armed forces, and the Manipur Naga People's Front (MNPF) claimed responsibility for the attack. Even today, more than two dozen groups of different communities or tribes are involved in the insurgency with the Nagas leading, followed by the Meiteis. The Kuki groups have been subdued for the time being, after coming to an agreement with the Centre and suspending their operations. The Chinese have been helping some of these groups in the past and it is suspected that China is involved even now.

In spite of the presence of the army in Manipur for decades, the situation is still the same. The model of operations needs to change, focusing on strengthening the local police so that they can lead the operations. The army should be withdrawn slowly, but I doubt whether it will leave the state as it has developed vested interests with permanent establishments in Manipur now. Somewhere, it is the failure of the Centre as it continues to use the army in such areas, without giving the local police more resources to lead the operations.

Central Industrial Security Force (CISF)

After some twists and turns, I got posted to the Central Industrial Security Force (CISF) in New Delhi as IG (Headquarters). In fact, my name had earlier been proposed to the PMO for a posting in the ITBP but someone influential got it instead. N.N. Vohra, the then Union Home Secretary (later Governor of J&K) helped me in getting IG CISF position then with his bold approach. He has helped many officers like me in service.

P.V. Narasimha Rao of the Congress had become the Prime Minister by then. No one ever thought that he would be placed in that position, but by default, he was elected as the leader of the Congress Party when Rajiv Gandhi was assassinated in May 1991. The general elections followed, resulting in a win for the Congress Party, which then made him the Prime Minister. In fact, he was almost retiring from politics and going back to his home in Hyderabad when fate intervened and brought him back. His unparalleled contribution in opening up the Indian economy, with the help of Manmohan Singh, then the Finance Minister, leading to the economic progress of the country, will always be remembered by posterity.

The CISF was raised in 1969, basically to guard industrial installations of the Government of India. Today, in addition to that duty, it is guarding airports, historical monuments, the metro stations in Delhi and offices of the Government of India. It also has a fire wing, disaster management units and a consultancy wing. Later, it also offered security consultancy to the private sector. Before I joined this force in 1993 as IG (Headquarters), four of my colleagues from the Delhi Police were posted there at the headquarters as DIGs. My senior in service, Gautam Kaul of the 1965 batch of the IPS was the DIG (Establishment), making it an unfortunate situation. He wasn't promoted due to some issue but it was a matter of embarrassment for both of us that even though I was his junior, I was his boss. I salute him for his maturity in dealing with these circumstances. He gave me full respect due to the rank and I also reciprocated with full regard and was always respectful to him in work and conduct. I was glad that he soon got what he deserved and was promoted.

The CISF is a well-structured organization with excellent officers and men. Some peculiar features of this force were that it charged a fee from the industrial units for its deployment and its formations were not in the form of battalions but need-based strength in units. Its own cadre officers were recruited through the civil services examination of the UPSC.

Much work had to be done to improve its functioning, which is a continuous process in all organizations. Huge construction work was needed at the National Industrial Service Academy at Hyderabad as well as other training institutions and for a battalion at Indira Puram in Ghaziabad near Delhi, apart from some other field formations. There was also the problem of a lack of promotions, especially at the SI level, as a very large number of personnel had been recruited in one go in a few batches. Apart from routine work, I contributed by giving many sanctions for construction at these and other places, streamlined administrative and financial aspects of the units, increased promotional posts for the ministerial staff, delegated powers, sent many officers of the SI rank on deputation to various organizations, some of whom got absorbed there and got promotions. A computer cell was also established to move with the times. The battalions of the CISF were not the same in strength, transport and other logistics, but everyone expected it to have fully equipped battalions like the BSF and CRPF when all these forces were deployed together in certain situations. With efforts, we were able to enhance the logistics part considerably, including transport, with sanctions from the government.

The CISF also celebrated its Silver Jubilee in 1994. During its celebrations, it got the President's Colours and a postage stamp in its honour was released, two special marks of recognition spearheaded by Gautam Kaul.

I was also able to write two books on industrial security in Hindi, including one in collaboration with DIG S.K. Singh and a book on human rights and the police, called *Manav Adhikar aur Police Bal* for the lower ranks. For this book, I was awarded a cash prize, the Govind Ballabh Pant Puraskar from the BPR&D and recognition from the National Human Rights Commission. Its Chairperson, Justice Ranganath Misra, in fact, released this book in the IIC. I also had the honour of presenting this book to the then President of India, Shankar Dayal Sharma, in Rashtrapati Bhawan when I visited him along with my family.

One of the memorable incidents relating to my books was meeting the famous writer, the late Khushwant Singh. I met him at his house in Sujan Singh Park near Khan Market and requested him to release my joke book. He refused but said that instead, he would do much more for me. His regular column, 'With Malice Towards One and All', published every week in leading newspapers, was very famous. He wrote an excellent review of my book, *Don't Laugh, We Are Police,* in his column the week following our meeting on 11 March 1995 and that day of publication happened to be my birthday. What a grand gift! Below is an excerpt from his review:

We do not associate wit or humour with policemen. Men in military uniforms do tell jokes against themselves but this is first time I have come across a compilation of jokes by a policeman against policemen. This is Bhushan Lal Vohra's *Don't Laugh, We Are Police* (Konark). The book was released by the dour-faced, macho mega-star of the police force K.P.S. Gill.

Vohra is no common or thana policeman. He took his MA in Economics from Delhi University before he joined the IPS in 1967. His wife Jyoti graduated from Miranda House before she married. They have three daughters. While serving in distant places like Manipur and Tripura as well as Punjab during its turbulent days he churned up books in Hindi and English on his experience as a police officer. Four years ago while posted as IG Manipur he wrote personal letters to senior contemporaries serving in different states to send him amusing anecdotes they had heard or were involved in. The first joke in the compilation is the response from a District Superintendent of Police:

Sir,

Sub: Police Jokes/Humour

I am directed to refer to Police HQ letter No. dated... on the above noted subject and to say that as far as this district is concerned the information is 'NIL'.

Yours faithfully,

Sd/-Superintendent of Police

To show my gratitude, I invited Khushwant Singh and his wife for dinner to my residence. He accepted but gave meticulous instructions regarding his timing of arrival, which scotch whisky he and his wife preferred and how many pegs, the timings of serving soup and dinner and then, the time of their departure. He came very informally dressed, not with proper Sikh headgear, but with a kind of handkerchief tied on his hair. The first thing he asked my wife on arrival was how we had met before our wedding. It was one of the most enjoyable evenings for me and my family.

During my stint in the CISF, I was also awarded the President's Police Medal for Distinguished Services. It was pinned on my chest by the then Prime Minister, H.D. Deve Gowda, during the anniversary parade of the CISF.

However, while I was still in Moti Bagh, there was a downturn in my health and there were other related financial issues, all of which made me miserable. Medicines and yoga were not of much help. Then my neighbour, a south Indian gentleman, and another friend, Shivendra Sinha, suggested that I do a 10-day long residential course in Vipassana meditation in the Chhatarpur area in Delhi, which was being conducted free. However, the condition was that I would have to live there for those 10 days. This course was based on the techniques of Gautam Buddha and taught in many centres by S.N. Goenka, with the help of assistant teachers in India and abroad. The rules were that a person who was going in for the course would have no contact with the outer world, no communication, no reading, no phone, or TV. Speaking even to a roommate was not allowed. It was only on the last day that talking was allowed. Breakfast was given in the morning, but simple vegetarian food was the fare once a day for the next meal. This is not the place to give too many details, but I must say one needs courage and forbearance to do this course.

I decided to try the Vipassana meditation, but when the course started, I wanted to run away. Somehow, I held on. One of the reasons was that I had announced from the rooftop that I was going for this tough course, so I knew that if I returned halfway, my family would laugh at me. By the sixth day, I started liking it and also the fact that half the journey was over was sufficient motivation for me to complete it. This was in 1993, when I was in the CISF. It changed the course of my life. I'm happier and healthier since then generally. It is not that all my problems went away, but my perception of them changed. Since then I have attended five more courses. My wife also followed later and has done three courses. On my recommendation, many of my friends have attended and benefitted. In fact, I recommend it to everyone.

In 1993, soon after joining the CISF, I had moved from Moti Bagh to Chanakyapuri to a ground floor flat, which had more space, with front and back lawns maintained well by our gardener Paras Ram. Archana was almost at the end of her postgraduation course in Business Economics from the South Campus of Delhi University, and Sonya had joined Lady Shri Ram College for History (Honours) at that time. Manika was still in school but soon joined Venkateswara College. After her postgraduation and being awarded a gold medal, Archana joined the corporate world. Sonya did a mass communications course from Jamia Millia Islamia after college and started working in the media. In September 1995, Archana got married to Rashi Mehra, a businessman from Defence Colony in Delhi. The marriage was solemnized in the CISF campus in Saket, which had a large compound. Her marriage brought so much joy to the family. Later, Archana moved from the corporate world to teaching economics in a university and did her PhD.

After Archana's marriage, we went to Moscow and London for a holiday with Sonya and Manika. We enjoyed the trip to Moscow and St Petersburg where we could see that even though Communism was waning, its stamp was still prominently there.

But life also has troubles and sorrow. A great misfortune was awaiting us. On 13 June 1997, my wife's youngest sister Geeta died along with her husband Narender and two sweet little daughters, Natasha and Neha, in a fire in the Uphaar Cinema tragedy in Green Park, Delhi, along with 55 other people. Earlier, they had never watched a film in the afternoon, but destiny took them there. We were in Mussoorie for a holiday in those days along with my father-in-law and mother-in-law. In the afternoon, I distinctly recall, I started feeling uncomfortable, some kind of premonition that something was wrong. Just then I got a call informing me about this terrible news. I didn't break the news to the family but gently told them that Geeta and her family were injured and had been taken to hospital. It was with great difficulty that I brought them to Delhi, each kilometre covered by the car seeming equivalent to a hundred miles. The family had hardly got over this tragedy, when my wife lost her uncle, younger than her father, and then my mother died on 29 October the same year. One felt like removing 1997 from the calendar—it was such a devastating period. But the heartbreak of losing Geeta and her family still remains and refuses to go away.

Reverting to my career, it was smooth till a boss who was difficult to work with joined. His conduct was almost unacceptable and he, too, was unhappy with most of the senior officers. I couldn't work in that atmosphere and apprehending that he may not give me a decent report in spite of my hard work, I preferred to quit and even leave Delhi at the cost of personal discomfort and that of the family. I opted for a posting in the BSF in J&K and was posted as IG BSF, Jammu. It was my second stint in the BSF after 1972–73, when I had commanded a BSF battalion in Faridkot. I alone went to J&K because according to the rules, we could retain our accommodation in Delhi.

Border Security Force (BSF), Jammu

Jammu was my new *karma bhumi* (land of action) for one year from September 1997 to September 1998. J&K was facing the brunt of Pakistan's continued hostility in the form of terrorists being regularly sent from across the border for subversive action. My task was to look after a portion of the international border with Pakistan in the Jammu region. Almost every night, there would be firing from the Pakistani side to give cover to those being sent to our side. Naturally, there was retaliatory firing from us. Every night, the sky was lit up with flames, sometimes even leading to killings of civilians and animals on both sides of the border. There were several battalions on the border, with many outposts.

The BSF there was under the operational control of the army, which meant that the Corps Commander based in Udhampur was my boss. I was like a Division Commander of the army and my colleague, who was looking after another portion of the International Border with Pakistan, was a Major General from the army.

Apart from trying to learn quickly, I also got a list of suggestions from the field officers about the work to be done, which was compiled in a booklet form and sent to the DG BSF at Delhi for action to be taken by the Force Headquarters. I acted on those areas that were administratively and financially within my powers. The jawans had some genuine difficulties which needed to be looked at to enable them to better their operational performance. For example, many border outposts (BOPs) had no drinking water facility nearby and especially during summer, jawans on duty would have to visit the nearby villages for water, thus leaving their outposts unmanned, which was not right. To solve this problem, we got them hand pumps so that they did not have to move away from their duty posts. Another suggestion came up that we should have *naka* or checkpoints, where jawans could take shelter in case of bad weather. These were designed and made. Then some BOPs urgently needed bunkers, which the army had but not the BSF, so we got those set up too.

An interesting story on this bunker episode is that in a meeting with the Corps Commander, when I mentioned the need for the bunkers and told him I had no bulldozer or other suitable machinery, he asked my army colleague, Major General Bhupinder Singh, to give me whatever was required. Soon after the meeting, I asked him how long it would take for the orders to be formally issued and for him to give me the machinery. He said, 'What written orders? Orders have been issued verbally and that is more than enough. You will get the machines tomorrow.' I was pleasantly surprised as we were all used to paperwork, even after verbal orders. I realized that the army functioned differently, and rightly so, as a war cannot be fought if written orders for implementation have to be given after every verbal order. It was a lesson worth learning and I tried to follow it to the extent possible later on.

A serious problem was the darkness on the border at night, giving an advantage to the Pakistanis when they wanted to send infiltrators. I was keen to have electricity there, but Pakistan would not allow us to erect poles and fix electric wires. Whenever we tried to do this, they would open fire, thus damaging the equipment. Once when I was returning from the border past midnight while passing through a village, I noticed a solar light on a pole giving sufficient light. This was nothing new, yet my brain flickered enough for me to realize that we could put up solar lights at the border and shooters of Pakistan Rangers would not be able to do much damage to these stand-alone poles. The rest, as they say, is history. We were able to put up many solar lights well within our budget by hiring a reputed company. However, we needed more lights. A bird then told me that the state government had purchased solar lights worth Rs 2 crore and these were lying waste in a big compound somewhere. I approached Chief Minister Farooq Abdullah, who used to come to our golf course once in a while to play, to give us those lights. He gladly obliged and we were able to put up this lighting up on a considerable length on the border. A few months later, I was surprised to see Pakistanis also putting up solar lights. During my meeting with my Pakistani counterpart later at the

Jammu border, I asked them to give us royalty for using this concept!

We had another serious problem of large numbers of Bangladeshis trying to infiltrate to Pakistan, either for a better life there or to go onwards towards Dubai and other cities. Touts were helping them by bringing them from Kolkata first to Amritsar and then from there to Jammu. Pakistanis would play mischief with them at times by retaining their women and pushing the men back. For us it was difficult to repatriate them as we had no funds, manpower and logistics for this purpose. So we would drop them in a truck more than a hundred miles away from the border. However, many of them would trek back.

A threat to life is a common situation in such postings. We had faced such situations in Manipur and Punjab and now it was the turn of J&K. While visiting the border one forenoon, as I was going from one BOP to another along with other officers, there was suddenly the sound of firing from the front, which was at some distance. We stopped and inquiries revealed that Pakistanis had started firing—they had got the information that senior officers were visiting the area. I was advised to go back, but I did not. Instead, I decided to stay put there till the firing stopped, but it took two hours or so for calm to prevail as heavy retaliation by our men followed. It was only when the firing stopped that we moved on. Going away from the scene would have been a blemish as Generals don't go back when faced with such situations.

Another time, just when my chopper was landing on an army helipad at Rajouri, a town about 155 kilometres from Srinagar (I had a chopper almost exclusively for myself to visit faraway places marked by difficult terrain), I heard a wireless conversation between a constable of the J&K Police and a terrorist. The terrorist told him, 'I'm seeing your big boss getting out of helicopter. I'll shoot him.' Obviously, he could see me from a hilltop as there were hills all around.

The constable told him, 'Do it and then come to the cremation ground in the afternoon to lay all your family members to rest.'

All this could be heard while the Brigadier and BSF officials were receiving me. They quickly took me to the car and drove me away. That is as close one can get to death at times. Receiving threatening phone calls and letters was routine.

As a part of maintaining a strong operational understanding, each year, BSF officials and the Pakistan Rangers would hold one meeting in Lahore and another one in Jalandhar or Delhi. It was for this meeting that I went to Lahore with my colleagues. Crossing over from the Wagah border, 32 kilometres from Amritsar and 24 kilometres away from Lahore, we were taken in the Pakistani force's excellent air conditioned cars. As we travelled, Liaison Officer Colonel Shaukat from the Pakistani Army completed a quote I began, saying: 'Is it correct that '*jine Lahore nai vekhya*... (One who has not yet seen Lahore...)'

He said, '...*O jamya-e-ni* (...has not been born).'

I had heard this saying from my parents. Lahore was an excellent city in all respects in the pre-Partition days and continues to be a bustling cosmopolitan city full of historic landmarks like the Lahore Fort dating from Mughal Emperor Akbar's reign, the Badshahi Mosque built in the time of Emperor Aurangzeb and heritage sites like the Shalimar Garden. Eateries abound in the markets of this sprawling city.

Pakistanis are very hospitable. My counterpart, Major General Saeed-ul-Hassan Zaidi, head of the Pakistani Rangers of Punjab, looked after us well in the Mess, but in the meeting, as expected, there was plenty of mutual fault-finding with the forces of each country.

Apart from the meeting, they made sure that we did some sight-seeing. They took us to Nankana Sahib Gurdwara, the birthplace of Guru Nanak Dev Ji. I was very keen to visit Panja Sahib, my birthplace. Zaidi kept on promising me a visit but never organized it. On the last day, just before our departure, I asked him why he didn't keep his promise. He was very frank, saying that when the Pakistan Rangers officials attended the meeting in Jalandhar, we did not allow them to visit Harminder Sahib in Amritsar and that was why he denied me the opportunity to see Panja Sahib! Mean of him I must say, but he had his own view. Later, I ensured that during their next visit to Jalandhar they were allowed to visit Harminder Sahib. Zaidi thanked me and assured me that I would be taken to Panja Sahib during our next visit to Pakistan. But by the time that meeting was held, I had left the BSF. So the regret of not being able to visit my birthplace remains and will perhaps be unfulfilled. I knew that even if I visited as a civilian, it was very risky for someone like me who has been in the police profession, as there was always the possibility landing in trouble. We could be suspected of being spies.

On the welfare front, a problem was that a large number of BSF personnel, including their relatives, wanted to go on a pilgrimage to Vaishno Devi, the religious site dedicated to the Mother Goddess who is said to grant all wishes. We were dependent on the CRPF, which was deployed at Katra, the base camp in the Trikuta Hills where the shrine is situated. Occasionally, there were problems with this arrangement, so as a solution, we opened a detachment at Katra, which is still there. Many of our relatives and friends, whom we had never expected to visit, came to meet us when they were on their way to Vaishno Devi. So at our house, we had a running kitchen and gave regular assistance for all their visits to the shrine. My staff officers D.S. Sandhu and C.P.S. Bali, both Deputy COs, were of great help in carrying out official duties and such arrangements.

I also visited Vaishno Devi quite a few times with my wife whenever she would come from Delhi. Once we were on the way to the shrine from Katra on foot when I got a message that there had been firing from Pakistani side. We were told that some civilians and animals had been killed on our side and that the villagers were very agitated. A big crowd had gathered and they were blaming the BSF for not taking any action against the Pakistanis. I had to rush back, leaving my wife to go ahead to the shrine alone. This was much against the belief that once one embarks on a journey to the shrine, one should never return after reaching halfway, but the call of duty was more important. We were able to calm the situation down after great efforts and assurances by our officers and men. And we retaliated after sometime at another location—a game commonly played.

An interesting incident illustrates how many happenings cannot be explained by any rationale and they seem to be the handiwork of God. One of my cousins from Ferozepur in Punjab rang me up one day, informing me that he had sent one of his junior-level employees to me for recruitment of his son in the BSF. I told him that in J&K, we can only recruit people domiciled in the state and that it was wrong of him to send him before talking to me. He apologized and told me that his employee was already on his way, so I should explain the situation to him when he arrived. When the person and his son met me the next evening at my bungalow, I conveyed my regret. As he was leaving, I asked his son whether he was skilled in any trade and the boy replied that he was a barber, his family profession. It occurred to me that tradesmen like him from any state in India can be recruited in the BSF. I told him to meet me the next morning. Meanwhile, I asked my principal staff officer, DIG H.K.S. Sehgal, whether there was any vacancy for a barber in the BSF. He replied in the negative but said that he would check up again and let me know in the morning.

When Sehgal met me the next morning, he seemed sad but with a touch of amusement. I was perplexed and asked him the reason for his twin expressions. He then informed me that one of our men had been killed that morning by Pakistani firing, which was sad news. The twist was that the dead man was a barber and had been killed in the most unlikely way, as he was not on the border, but was only shaving a constable under another tree close by. The bullet struck against a tree and turned straight towards him, killing him instantaneously! So there was no vacancy till 5 a.m. that day for a barber, but this sad incident did cause one and the position of a barber in the BSF went to the fellow who had come to me from Ferozepur last evening. How can you explain such things except by saying that these are the ways of God? Readers may recall another similar episode that I have mentioned earlier when I was in the BPR&D.

During this period, I used to visit Srinagar quite often as the coordination meetings were mostly held there with civilian authorities and other seniors visiting from Delhi.

We had a BSF school in the campus, which was doing very well with many civilian children attending this school. I conducted some courses on soft skills for officers and their families. A 10-day course on Vipassana meditation was also organized in the school campus. While there, I learnt a bit of golf on the campus' golf course from an instructor who held the rank of a Head Constable. It was all going very well. In Jammu, I could reconnect with one of my seniors, T.R. Kalra of the J&K cadre, my erstwhile colleague in BPR&D, who had settled in Jammu after retirement.

I had brought my mother from Delhi to Jammu for some time to stay with us. When I accompanied her back to Delhi, she fell seriously sick. She was admitted to Jaipur Golden Hospital in Delhi, and my wife and I were at her bedside when she breathed her last on 29 October 1997. It was a big setback, a huge loss.

Next year, I took leave and went with the family to the Andaman & Nicobar Islands for a break. During my absence, terrorists killed 26 Hindus in Prankote village in the Udhampur district of Jammu. The blame for not taking enough defensive measures was put on the BSF, even though we were not looking after that area. I was summoned back from leave and travelled with L.K. Advani, the then Union Home Minister, to Jammu in the BSF plane. There was a lot of hue and cry over the tragic incident and even though I could prove that the BSF was not at fault, my efforts were in vain. The army and the police pinned the blame on us. It was actually a grey area and could have been the fault of the local police or the army whose job it was to earmark the areas of responsibility.

Anyway, the end result was that the DG BSF, who was unhappy with some steps I had taken at the border, such as construction of *naka* points and installing handpumps, etc. for the jawans, found this an opportunity to post me out of BSF and wrote to the Ministry of Home Affairs, asking for my repatriation to my cadre. When I got to know of it, I met the Union Home Minister to present my side of the story. He was convinced that I was not wrong and took the decision to move me to the National Security Guard (NSG) in Delhi as the IG (Headquarters) instead of sending me back to my cadre.

Overall, my tenure in J&K was excellent and a great learning experience. Carrying out my duties gave me satisfaction and a sense of fulfilment. Though the end was not glorious, it worked well for me in the end because I moved back to Delhi to be with my family and gain experience of working in the NSG.

National Security Guard (NSG)

The NSG was raised in the wake of the 1984 Operation Blue Star in Punjab, and the high collateral damage to the Golden Temple, and civilian and military casualties. It has done stellar work in Punjab, J&K and elsewhere since its inception. Popularly known as the Commando outfit, it had earned quite a few laurels for its work. It is a mix of army and police personnel, almost in equal proportion and drawn from different units of each side. I was the IG (Headquarters) and my counterpart from the army was the IG (Operations). It was a great learning and working experience. Its logistics and functioning were much ahead of the other Central Armed Police Forces (CAPFs). The uniform, which I also wore, was grey. I also started getting free rations on the pattern of fringe benefits given to army officers. Its training centre and operating units were mainly located in Manesar near Gurgaon (Gurugram) in Haryana.

I saw there was quite a bit to do after watching the force's extensive exercises of different kinds and requirements on the administrative side like allowances, procurement, induction of manpower, and so on. Apart from handling hostage situations, it was also put on security duties of VVIPs, and later some of its units had to be located in different regions of India when situations demanded quick movement by the NSG as transportation from Delhi to far-off places took time. The multiple attacks by Pakistani terrorists on Mumbai on 26 November 2008 were one such instance. The NSG commandos were given charge of the operations to fight the terrorists and did so successfully.

Regarding getting manpower for NSG on deputation from Central and state police forces, we were falling short. One day, it just occurred to me to tap Assam Rifles—the oldest paramilitary force raised in the North-East in 1835 with a different name, Cachar Levy, and its manpower was always deployed only in that region. I guessed that there would be many personnel who would like to serve in Delhi as perhaps quite a few would have been recruited to this force from northern India. I flew to Shillong in Meghalaya where the Assam Rifles headquarters are and met the then DG of Assam Rifles to ask him to send some of his junior ranks on deputation to us. He was delighted as, indeed, there were many Assam Rifles personnel recruited from northern India who were keen to serve nearer home. Many others also wanted a change. And as they say, the rest is history. It was a win-win situation for both the NSG and Assam Rifles. It helped many to be nearer home for some years, and this arrangement continues even today.

The Kargil war had taken place at that time. It was won by India and Pakistan had to suffer a humiliating retreat from the hills. The NSG also got some credit even though it was not involved in the war. I remember being invited to a function to felicitate the armed forces on this victory. I think the reason was that we had a large contingent of army personnel working in the NSG.

On the family front, a joyful event took place. I became a grandfather when Archana was blessed with a daughter in January 1999. As I distributed sweets in office, I asked my counterpart, Major General Hoshiyar Singh, who was already a grandfather, what would change for me now. He said, 'Sir, you are a grandfather now, and you have a granddaughter. That's what has changed' while emphasizing the word 'grand'. It was well described.

Sometime later my tenure ended and I had to proceed to Manipur, back to my cadre, after serving in the NSG from September 1998 to December 1999. At the time of my departure, Nikhil Kumar was my DG. He was also my first boss in the Delhi Police when I was his ASP and he was the SP of the North District.

By this time Atal Bihari Vajpayee of the BJP had become the Prime Minister and continued till 2004 when the Congress Party won the elections. After that, in a coalition called the United Progressive Alliance (UPA), Manmohan Singh became the Prime Minister till 2014 when the BJP won a landslide victory, repeating it in 2019 with Narendra Modi as the Prime Minister. He continues as such at the time of completing this book.

Chapter 10

Tripura Again

Back to Manipur, I was promoted to the rank of a DGP, a three-star police general, the highest rank one can aspire for after joining the IPS, and it was a big satisfaction for me to have reached that level. I was posted to the Police Housing Corporation, but only for a short while. After that I was posted as the DGP Sikkim. I was keen to go there but a twist in fate took me to Tripura as the DGP instead, in the month of May 2000. The state was facing a serious insurgency for over two decades. My taking over there was like a baptism by fire as just two days before I joined, 20 poor Bengalis had been killed by insurgents of All Tripura Tiger Force (ATTF) in Bagber village in West Tripura district.

At that time, it was the worst affected state in the North-East due to insurgency. Gone were the peaceful days when I had served earlier there as an SP in 1973–75. The genesis was that Bengali Hindus had captured the state by their sheer numbers when they migrated to Tripura after the formation of East Pakistan, which later got converted into Bangladesh. They fled to Tripura because of the atrocities committed on them by the Muslim majority in Bangladesh. Many came from the region called Chakla Roshnabad—as the Tripura Maharaja was the zamindar there, it was natural for them to take shelter in his state. The tribals to whom the land originally belonged became a minority and were driven to the hills. They became inferior inhabitants in their own land, which they resented. Since peaceful methods did not work to give them back their due, they took up weapons supported by Pakistan and later even the Bangladesh intelligence agencies.

Two insurgent outfits, the National Liberation Front of Tripura (NLFT) and the ATTF, were dominant at that time. Killings of Bengalis, abductions, landmines, arson and other violence were the order of the day. There was some retaliation by the Bengalis also, which inflamed the communal situation as well. Here again, the Central government was responsible to quite an extent for the situation as it had no time and policy for handling the situation properly, except for sending forces and money, and the local politicians mostly being Bengalis with some sprinkling of tribals, were finding it difficult to handle the situation. With an easy access to Bangladesh just across the border for their bases of operations and shelters, the insurgents were having a field day. They were mostly in the hills, getting support from the local tribals.

It was a tough situation which was not coming under control. The blame game was in full gear, with the state government and bureaucracy blaming the police and the CRPF and vice versa. The common man was under pressure with threats all the time apart from the loss of lives, property and anything of value. To pay ransom for the huge number of people who were kidnapped, many had to sell their land and valuables. The state government would complain that the Central government was not helping and the Central government felt that the state was not doing enough to control the situation.

In any such circumstances, the political will to sort out a problem or not is most important. At that time, the plus point was that Chief

Minister Manik Sarkar of the CPM wanted to sort out the issue and improve the situation, as did V. Thulasidas, the Chief Secretary, whom I knew as he had joined as an IAS probationer during my earlier stint in Tripura, George Podipara, the IG CRPF, whom also I had known earlier as he was my commandant in Delhi in the CRPF when I was DIG (Range) and Lieutenant General (Retd.) K.M. Seth, who was the Governor. With some effort I was able to strike a good equation with them and worked seriously to restore some order.

The first requisite was to understand the situation on the ground for which I did extensive touring and spoke to many people inside and outside, including the media. Regular kidnappings for ransom from different parts of the state were always in the news and gave a bad name to the police and the state. My conclusion was that the Tripura Police was a very fine police force but needed to be strengthened in a big way to lead the operations and achieve success in containing violence, which is the basic charter of the police and the security forces in any insurgency situation. It is not their task to solve basic issues. There was no army there though there were three battalions of the Assam Rifles deployed on the ground, which was, in a way, a positive factor as the police was free to lead the operations, which is how it should be.

A corner in my heart told me that it is indeed possible to control the situation, but the roadmap had to be figured out. But these were initial days and I was doubtful about my capability to do the needful. At this juncture, George Podipara, IG CRPF, bolstered my confidence. One day when we were travelling and I shared my doubts with him, he said, 'Sir, I know that you can and will do it. I have seen your functioning in the CRPF where you achieved a lot, and I'm confident. And, of course, I'll do whatever you ask me to do.'

With sustained thinking, discussions with officers and inputs from the ground level for which I talked to over a hundred different ranks of police from different departments, a broad strategy started appearing slowly on the horizon. Our media friends suggested that kidnappings should be handled on priority as they were making the life of the people miserable and gave a bad name to the police. In this case and otherwise also, there were two options on the table—either to start tackling the situation from the inner side of the state and then go to the outer areas or work in the reverse order. The latter option was chosen and we experimented with a decision to control the regular kidnappings from the Dumbur Lake in Kanchanpur sub-division. The operation was led by the brave DSP, Monoranjan Debbarma, and was successful. It was tough to organize logistics like manpower, boats and weapons but it was done. We tasted blood with this first success. The steps taken here to check kidnappings became a template for other areas and slowly, we were able to almost stop kidnappings over a period of time—to the huge relief of everyone.

The entire credit for this initial success went to Monoranjan Debbarma who offered to go all out to curb kidnapping, planning and executing his strategy well. Unfortunately, we lost him in an encounter later on, which was a huge blow. That day is still etched in my memory as a painful loss. I didn't eat food after paying homage to him and the local press mentioned that I was a distraught chief that day. I went to his village for his cremation and later we renamed the police stadium in Agartala after him.

Though losing men in such battles is part of the game, it still hurts. Another such big hurt was on 20 August 2000 when a group of NFLT militants ambushed and killed 20 jawans of the 7th Battalion of the Tripura State Rifles (TSR), the armed wing of the Tripura Police, at Hirapur under Takarjala police station. It was heart-rending to pay homage to 20 bodies, wrapped in white cloth and lying in a line, before being despatched to their respective homes.

Reverting to Monoranjan Debbarma, I recall an incident in the

Dumbur Lake area while he was still alive. He was keen that I go to the lake myself to see the improvement in the situation. We started one evening in fine weather in two mechanized boats along with the CO of the TSR and some jawans from Rashyabari in south Tripura. After some time one boat developed a snag that made it stall. We left it and shifted to the other boat. However, that also stopped moving after some time! It was getting dark. By a strange coincidence, the wireless set with us also became defective. Stranded in the middle of the very big lake, we anxiously looked for help. To our relief, a civilian boat came along and we asked the people in it to carry us to the nearest island called Dakmura. That boat could accommodate about six to seven people, so the CO, DSP, about four jawans and I headed towards that island which was inhabited.

Very reluctantly, Monorajan confided that it was a well-known hideout of one of the insurgent groups. That naturally worried us. For them to have the DGP of the state for slaughter on a plate would have been the best thing to happen operationally and for publicity. Anyway, we tried to calm our nerves, stood guard with our weapons in a carefully chosen corner and looked desperately for help, with tension overwhelming us. After some time, we noticed a big boat carrying people and merchandise passing from close by and we managed to get it to stop. We boarded it and, to our relief, reached the safety of the mainland in the early hours of the morning.

Reverting to tackling insurgency, I was gradually convinced that we would be able to handle the situation. The next big task was to convince the officers and other ranks of the police force. It took time, but slowly, I was able to convince them by exhorting them to take action at all available opportunities. Of course, we needed lot of wherewithal to achieve success, which we ultimately arranged. Slowly, we started achieving success against the insurgents and finally the Tripura Police was able to turn the corner decisively. The press lauded our work.

On this success of counter-insurgency operations led by the Tripura Police, I later wrote a book, *Tripura's Bravehearts*, published by Konark, the publisher of this book as well. I presented a copy of this book to the then Prime Minister Manmohan Singh on 1 July 2011 soon after its publication and he lauded the work of the Tripura Police. Those interested in knowing the details may go through the book, but here, I will briefly mention the steps taken in our fightback.

After tackling kidnappings, our attention was turned to operations against the insurgents and the security and safety of the populace, especially the Bengali population. A mere look at the map of Tripura showed that the insurgents were operating from the hills where there was no police presence as all the police stations and posts were on the main roads. I was convinced that we should move into the hills. So I called a meeting of all the senior officers and asked them their views. The opinion was divided but I stuck to my decision of moving in. Then I asked for volunteers who would open the first camp. To my pleasant surprise, CO Joydev Das of the 2nd TSR Battalion, beyond 50 in age, who had risen from ranks, volunteered. He set up a camp in a place called Panjirai in the south district. I visited it and stayed overnight in one of the locations of his battalion.

However, we needed manpower in a big way to move into the hills. The sanctioned strength of the police was less than required and much of our manpower was concentrated on VIP security duties and in security camps in some villages and areas that had witnessed killings. So the police were somewhat handicapped in taking any proactive steps against the insurgents.

The government was kind enough to sanction more manpower to increase the strength of the existing police stations as well as increase the number of police stations and TSR battalions. We also got a few India Reserve Battalions raised by the state but funded by the Centre. We began taking measures to establish TSR camps in the areas dominated by the insurgents. Even the headquarters of some battalions were relocated in the interiors. We also managed to get four companies of the TSR as peace companies to guard the ongoing projects because we knew that insurgents extorted money from the contractors and had to be prevented from doing so.

But the biggest success was to persuade the Chief Minister to appoint a large number of Special Police Officers (SPOs) under the Police Act. It took time but he finally agreed. We appointed a large number of unemployed youth, and those tribal boys who were helping insurgents in the hills, as SPOs with a fixed salary of Rs 1500, gave them some training and .303 Rifles. We established many camps with a strength ranging from 10–30 personnel with a regular police Havildar or someone of the same rank as the in-charge of the camp. The Chief Minister agreed because I told him that in this way he could oblige cadres of the CPM, a suggestion that clicked! However, when I said one day that he was not agreeing to the appointment of non-CPM people and, therefore, it seemed he was raising a Red Army, he didn't like it, naturally. Additionally, the functioning of the Home Guards was revitalized by weeding out the dead wood and replacing it with young blood.

Two newly raised TSR battalions were also trained in counter-insurgency operations in the army's Counter Insurgency and Jungle Warfare School at Vairengte in Mizoram. Later, we opened our own training school in Dhalai district for this purpose. Accommodation, training, weapons, transport, communications and other logistics were arranged on a war footing. For accommodation, we established semi-pucca iron structures which were more durable than the normal bamboo *basha*s (structures).

In no time, we managed contact with the insurgents at many places as they were taken by surprise. Increased intelligence and cooperation from the people in the hills and elsewhere bolstered our success, supported by the bureaucracy, politicians and the media. Our intelligence unit revitalized itself, including launching psychological warfare against the insurgents. The extensive touring that I undertook in the jungles on foot with other officers raised the morale of the forces. Once in November 2001, I walked for about 30 kilometres through the jungles and difficult mountain terrain to visit one of the remote TSR camps at a place called Rabanpara in Dhalai district. I visited each police station, sometimes by surprise, and gave them all the resources needed to fight the situation. They also knew that they would be held accountable. For improving firing standards, an indoor firing range was also procured. The communications system was revitalized by connecting all police stations with a wireless set-up in each moving VIP, filling the gaps that existed earlier.

The Central government also chipped in. We got some money and weapons, transport, other equipment under the modernization grant. Surrender-cum-Rehabilitation schemes were launched and operated, with the result that quite a few surrenders took place. A camp for those who gave up arms was established to stay there safely or learn skills that would help them join the mainstream.

So the battle was on. The ambushes, the encounters, the attacks went on, but slowly, the violence graph came down and the number of insurgents killed or captured with weapons increased.

In the process of implementing these strident measures, normal policing was not neglected. It was made effective and, where necessary, some new police stations and police posts were set up. When I wanted some policemen to be transferred to outlying areas from Agartala and vice versa, it transpired that most of the recruits in the police were from Agartala and not from outlying areas. Connections in the capital were used to corner the jobs, so they were reluctant to go out. That imbalance in recruitment was corrected and young men from poor families in all sub-divisions were located and recruited. There was a streamlining of administration and incentives like the DG's Commendation Disc for outstanding performance were introduced, besides establishing a Forensic Science Laboratory.

On the welfare front, speedy allotment of jobs in the government, preferably in the police department, within a week for the next of kin of the policemen killed in action was always assured. I visited the family of each person killed while on duty, in any part of the state. A departmental bus was started from Agartala to Guwahati for the welfare of the police personnel belonging to other states going on leave, and many more such steps taken. With an improvement in the situation, we started the *Tripura Police Week*, a police magazine, and other ventures that could encourage the police. In all, we took more than 100 steps as tabulated by A.K. Shukla, the then DIG (Range), on my request when I was writing the book on Tripura. He had said that it was 100 not out!

Men of all ranks of the Tripura Police worked very hard. There is not enough space here to mention all the names, but still I would like to convey my appreciation to some officers such as Salim Ali, IG (Law and Order), Kishore Jha, IG (Intelligence), Dilipjit Deb Barma, DIG (Administration), A.K. Shukla, DIG (Range), Kuldeep Kumar, DIG (Operations) and the SPs, Anurag of the West District, Puneet Rastogi of the North District, T.B.Roy of the South District, Khatrojoy Reang of the Dhalai district, S.S. Chaturvedi, SP (Intelligence), D. Gautam, SP (Operations), Amitabh Kar SP (Communications) and the COs, S.K. Darlong of the 1st Battalion (TSR) and Joydev Das of the 2nd Battalion (TSR), and many other efficient, brave officers, including many distinguished SHOs.

An excellent supporting hand was given by the late George Podipara, IG (CRPF), V. Thulasidas, the Chief Secretary, other officers in the Secretariat, especially in Home and Finance, and, of course, Chief Minister Manik Sarkar, who himself used to interact with the officials at the police station level. Occasionally, we had differences on some issues but he was graceful in finding a solution. And at least at my level, there was no interference in my work from him though I know that he had other ways of getting work done.

I did an unusual thing in writing a letter of appreciation to the Chief Minister once, something which is normally written to subordinates. He must have been the first Chief Minister to receive such a letter and I would have been the first DGP, perhaps, to write such a letter to a Chief Minister! It amused him a little though I'm sure he would have liked it.

However, one day I had a serious tiff with him. The government had taken away some powers of the police department which I wanted back. By coincidence, we were both travelling by air from Kolkata, where we had gone for some work, to Agartala, seated side by side in economy class (though we were both entitled for business class, the CPM cadre always travel economy class and made us do the same). I slowly broached the subject with him. Normally a cool person, he became furious and raised his voice while countering my point. I don't know why but I also got worked up and increased my decibel level while arguing with him. Soon I realized where I was, stopped my argument, apologized to him and kept quiet thereafter. Except for a little chat later, to restore normalcy, we both went to our respective offices after landing.

I was disturbed, so I called him and sought an appointment. He told me to meet him at 7 p.m. that evening. When I met him, I apologized again for raising my voice during the flight. I also told him to relieve me of my duties by giving me two months' leave, and appoint someone else in my place as I could not work with such an attitude of the government towards the police department where some powers had been taken away. He calmed me down, relented and agreed to our demand. It was so nice of him.

On another occasion, we wanted to improve the Chief Minister's security at his residence by bringing in some minor modifications and additional lighting, but he would not allow it in spite of my personal discussion with him. When all efforts failed, I wrote to the Chief Secretary, stating that due to the insurgency in the state if something happened to the Chief Minister, the police department would not be responsible because the Chief Minister was not agreeing to our suggestions. I pointed out that he was vulnerable as was the security front at his residence. The Chief Secretary took the letter to the Chief Minister and at once we got the approval for beefing up his security.

Governor Seth was also supportive of our efforts. From the Central government, Gopal Pillai, the then Joint Secretary dealing with the North-East and later as the Union Home Secretary, was very helpful. The intelligence agencies, the IB and the Research and Analysis Wing (RAW), also helped us a lot.

But I couldn't resist telling Vajpayee, the then Prime Minister, during the conference of DGPs, about the discriminatory treatment of the police by the state governments regarding modernization grants for police released by the Centre. Mostly, they were not giving their share of the matching grants, and some even were not releasing the grants received from the Centre.

Interestingly, once some leaders of the main Opposition party came to see me for some work. They conveyed their compliments for our police work but told me that in public, being in the Opposition, they would continue criticizing the government and the police! I didn't mind as that was their job.

The main thing was that the people of the state were happy. Safety and security for the populace is always hugely welcomed. The local and Kolkata media lauded the work of the Tripura Police, but the news of its success took time to reach Delhi. For me, this gave great personal and professional satisfaction and, in a way, was my finest hour.

I can't claim that the insurgency came to an end at that time but it was controlled considerably. My distinguished successors did the rest of the job in later years. However, the genuine grievances of the tribals remain and need to be sorted out. I had mentioned this to the Chief Minister and all others who mattered and were willing to hear. But I suppose, ultimately, all-round development along with the political will to find solutions will slowly make them move on with time.

On the family front, my second daughter Sonya got married to Rajnish on 8 October 2000 in Delhi. She had completed her course in Mass Communications from Jamia Millia Islamia and worked with the media for many years. She now owns a media company. Rajnish is in the corporate world and has steadily been moving up the ladder since then. A strange coincidence is that Sonya was born during my first posting to Tripura in 1974 and got married during my second posting there!

Four of us, my wife, her parents who were visiting us, and I visited Dhaka and were received and looked after very well by the personnel of Bangladesh Rifles during my posting in Tripura. It was a memorable visit. We also had a social life in Agartala during my posting though there was not much time for this activity. We lived in the earmarked bungalow of the DGP in Kunjaban with quite a few excellent people to look after us, especially Debnath who was with me during my first stint there about a quarter of a century earlier. Archana, with her husband Rashi, Sonya and Manika visited us. Shreya, my granddaughter, was happy playing with rabbits all day long and drank milk only after she could see a cow, which at times took a little long as a cow in the vicinity had to be located! In March 2002, Archana was blessed with a baby boy, Vansh. My wife and I were now proud grandparents of two grandchildren and what a joy it was!

Since I felt I'd done my bit in Tripura, I started looking for a posting in Delhi as I had barely two years of service left and wanted to be there in time to plan my post-retirement settlement. I got posted as the DG (Civil Defence) in the Home Ministry with the Government of India. As a parting gesture, the Chief Minister and Chief Secretary lauded my work and the Chief Minister was very gracious in sending a lovely gift to my wife on the eve of our departure. I have always been an admirer of both of them.

Chapter 11

Civil Defence and a Border Force

Back to Delhi, my office as DG (Civil Defence) was on the first floor of Jaisalmer House, the building in which I had started my government career way back in 1964—thus life came full circle. This department, which was very important at the time of its establishment after the conflict with China in 1962, had become a very unimportant and unnoticeable one by the time I joined. The few staff members were spread over in the building and some outlying staff were posted to Kolkata. There was no proper sanctioned strength of the office and not even a car of its own for the DG (Civil Defence).

In the wake of the Chinese aggression, quite a few departments like the ITBP, the then Special Service Bureau and now the SSB, Civil Defence, among others were established. When the Civil Defence department was set up at that time, the officials sought the help of British officers familiar with civil defence work during the Second World War, and a senior Major General of the Indian army was tasked to head it. The aim of the department was to prepare itself to serve the government and the army during war time. Raising of Home Guards and Fire Services in the states along with Civil Defence volunteers was a part of its mandate. This work was done with gusto. Its then DG used to sit in North Block in a room almost next to the room of the Union Home Secretary. However, over the years, there were no wars, especially after 1971, and the department also faded away, sitting in a nondescript corner with many officers in the Home Ministry, including the minister, not knowing that such a department even existed.

I took upon myself the task of rejuvenating the department. We moved to a new consolidated office in R.K. Puram, rewrote manuals, designed new formats of certificates for appreciation and for medals of the government, raised the emoluments of Civil Defence volunteers who were still getting only Rs 10 per day as an allowance in some states. The daily wages of Home Guards were raised in many states after great efforts. L.K. Advani, the then Home Minister, was gracious enough to earmark a percentage of a modernization grant for Home Guards in the states. The Fire Services in the states were revitalized by first calling a meeting of the Fire Services chiefs in Delhi and later in Goa, and sorted many issues, including authorizing each one to hold promotion courses at their own locations rather than sending each one to the National Fire Service College at Nagpur. This speeded up considerably delayed promotions. The National Civil Defence College at Nagpur was also infused with new life.

Reviving the past practice, I wore the prescribed grey uniform and visited each state to meet the Chief Ministers personally to exhort them to look after the Civil Defence and Home Guards personnel, to improve the functioning of the Fire Services in their states and increase and update their allowances, training and equipment. I also asked them to claim their reimbursement money from us, which was being surrendered each year. Mostly, there were encouraging results. It was a great pleasure to meet some Chief Ministers, especially those who gave me an exclusive patient hearing. These were Narendra Modi of Gujarat (now the Prime Minister of India), Tarun Gogoi of

Assam and A.K. Antony of Kerala. The Maharashtra and Bihar Chief Ministers raised the allowances of the volunteers considerably. Some of my batchmates in those days were posted as DGs (Civil Defence) in their respective states and all were doing excellent work, including S.M. Cairae in Jharkhand and P.K. Senapati in Odisha. I started calling them and other DGs for meetings to Delhi.

A new flag was made for the department and was inaugurated by Home Minister Advani in Vigyan Bhawan where we also started an annual meeting of the heads of these departments from the states for an interaction on the lines of the annual conference of the IB. The Home Ministry was very supportive, including the then Home Secretary, N. Gopalaswami, and Joint Secretary, R.K. Singh, who is currently the Union Minister for Power. A big publicity campaign was launched to let people know of the Civil Defence organization and exhorting them to join. There were many enthusiastic responses from all over the country. I also visited France to know about their civil defence functioning and South Korea to attend a conference.

A need was felt to have a separate Disaster Management Force and I wrote the first noting giving a brief outline on how to go about raising it, leading ultimately to the setting of the National Disaster Management Authority (NDMA) and the National Disaster Management Force (NDRF) consisting of two battalions each on deputation from the main paramilitary forces. My experience in the NSG earlier was helpful when I wrote these proposals. I am so glad that these organizations have come up and are doing excellent work in the country and abroad, earning laurels.

Director General of Sashastra Seema Bal (SSB)

In between, I was also given the charge of DG (SSB). Though it turned out to be only for a few months, it was a rich experience and I could humbly contribute quite a bit. This force was declared a border guarding force in uniform and was tasked to look after the Indian borders with Nepal and Bhutan on the recommendation of the reports of the Kargil Review Committee and Group of Ministers set up after the Kargil war in 1999. However, administrative and financial powers, such as the sanction of construction works at new posts along the borders, etc., of officers at various levels were not moving with times, unlike in the BSF, CRPF and other forces. Since I had served in those organizations, I brought these powers at par with those organizations. It was a revolutionary change, according to some officers.

One day, I was told by Jyoti Swaroop Pandey, IG (Lucknow), that about 60 constables had not got the senior scale called the Assured Career Progression (ACP) scale that they were entitled to. I immediately asked the Delhi-based CO who confirmed it and said that the figure was more than 100. The reason was that they had not undergone the mandatory two-month training course. They couldn't do the training course as the training academy at Sapri in Himachal Pradesh did not have enough capacity to accommodate all of them. The constables were suffering as a consequence, for no fault of their own. I could guess that a similar situation existed in other battalions also. I ordered a count and by the next day discovered that the figure was more than 3,000 constables! Shocked, I called both the IG (Personnel) and IG (Training) and asked them to rectify this. I suggested that they could reduce the training period to two weeks from two months and conduct the training in each battalion itself, with a target of issuing the ACP to all eligible constables in a month's time. The needful was done, barring exceptions as some constables were on leave or for other reasons. But the measures taken became an eye-opener and soon other cadres in SSB also clamoured for similar changes, which were then carried out.

For the border outposts and other establishments, money was released for the infrastructure while simultaneously raising the financial powers of the officers in the field. Similarly, some other steps were taken to improve the efficiency of the force besides looking after the welfare of men. It gave me great satisfaction to do this and I am so glad that even today many of the old stalwarts of the SSB compliment me for the work I did. Actually, it was nothing unusual and could be expected of any chief.

Post-Retirement Plans

When about one year for my retirement on 31 March 2004 was left, I started thinking of my post-retirement plans. The family in the meanwhile was growing. Sonya was blessed with a baby girl, Tia. Manika was studying law in the Law Faculty of Delhi University. She met Anuj there and they decided to get married on 1 February 2004, two months before my retirement. So God was kind and taking care of my family front.

I had to first think of where to stay. I had two options—the house in Bharat Nagar, my ancestral property that was lying vacant after the demise of my parents, and the other one was the DDA flat we owned in Saket. Considering all factors, we decided to shift to Saket and asked the tenant to vacate it on 1 January 2004 so that we could renovate it before shifting.

I also had to think of how to keep myself busy. Since I had been used to an active life in the police for almost four decades, it was unimaginable to sit at home and do nothing. I was always fond of training and while in service itself, I had started training workshops on soft skills for officers from my CISF days. So I decided to work as a trainer in these skills. I went to the Dale Carnegie Centre of Excellence in Manhattan in New York to attend a few courses at my own expense to hone my skills. My wife and I stayed there with Divya and Deepak Aggarwal, the daughter and son-in-law of my dear friend P.K. Gupta. They were very gracious hosts and we still remember their hospitality.

After marriage, Manika moved to Model Town. Both of them are practising lawyers, and Anuj is the Additional Standing Counsel of the Delhi government in the High Court. We were free from the primary responsibility of marrying off our daughters, and had given them the best of education and whatever comforts we could afford, which though frugal by all standards, were sufficient for them. We tried to make them responsible citizens and they have done us proud. We are very lucky that all our three girls are settled in Delhi–NCR and we can meet them, their families and grandchildren anytime without much travel.

Retirement

I finally hung up my boots on 31 March 2004 and the office staff gave me an emotional farewell. My batchmate S. Ramakrishnan, Ramu as I call him, was DG (Civil Defence) in the Delhi government. He organized a farewell parade and dinner for me, which was attended by my Delhi-based batchmates and their families. During my farewell speech, I thanked God, my parents, my family, friends, countless other men and women and my country for giving me so much in life that I never deserved. With pride, I also told the gathering that I was wearing the same tunic and shirt that comprised the uniform I had got stitched in 1967 at Mount Abu, together with a tie, during my initial training—with the same measurements. With moist eyes, I left the parade ground, finally saying goodbye to a long career in the police—a profession that I fell in love with after joining and will remain attached to as long as I live. I am still a policeman at heart and miss my uniform occasionally. It was such a great opportunity to serve the people with my limited capability and in all humility.

Chapter 12

Hanging up My Boots

Renovating our two-bedroom small flat in Saket constructed by the DDA, which is what I could afford, was an intensive exercise that was undertaken by my wife from January 2004 onwards. It was completed well in time before our entitlement to government accommodation at Chanakyapuri ended by the end of November that year. We moved into the flat to begin a new life in a much smaller space and totally strange surroundings. It was a different life without perks and privileges or uniformed men and chauffeur-driven cars. On the very first day, we had a skirmish with a neighbour over parking issues. He was not willing to withdraw and was rather aggressive. I rang up K.K. Paul, the then Commissioner of Delhi Police, to help, which he did. The neighbour did not continue with his complaints but, unfortunately, remains unfriendly till date, which was a heavy price to be paid. But these are the perils of living in civilian localities.

Becoming a Trainer

Picking up the threads of life, I decided to start my work of conducting training workshops. An office was hired, an employee appointed and a website developed for my company called M5Trainers. I even attended a course at the National Institute of information Technology (NIIT), Saket with 18-year-olds as my classmates to upgrade my computer skills, learn about Microsoft Word, and so on. My first workshop held at the India Habitat Centre was well attended and I earned a reasonable amount of money. This was followed by a few more training sessions but then I lost the energy for marketing, which was necessary for publicity. A stroke of luck helped me at this point. I had gone to Baroda to do a training workshop with a Gujarat government firm, courtesy my friend D.D. Tuteja who had retired as the Police Commissioner of Baroda and was once my colleague in the Railway Board as an Assistant. While returning from Baroda, on the flight I met Shyam Bang, the Executive Director of a reputed pharmaceutical company with headquarters in Noida (UP), adjoining Delhi, who asked me to do training courses for their staff in one of their many plants. I also got offers from other companies to conduct courses at their locations at their expense. So I closed down my office and concentrated on doing these workshops, enjoying sharing my experience and making good money, without worries about marketing and running an office.

Later, Bang asked me to look into the security of their plants all over India as they were not happy with the security consultant who was working for them. Reluctantly, I took over this task and from then on, began getting security work from elsewhere as well. For over a decade starting from 2005, I was doing both these jobs.

Meanwhile, my wife and I were keen to do some service to society. While I was in the police, I had once gone to Jharkhand and happened to visit an impoverished village in the interior. I was told that two or three of the women in a family shared the only sari they had and they went out of the house in turns, wearing that single sari! I had then decided to start an NGO named 'Vastradan' after my retirement to collect spare old clothes from homes and distribute these among the poor. We got our NGO registered in 2005 and have continued to contribute to society in this way. By now, we have collected and distributed over a million clothes in different parts of India including during disasters and have many partners, such as paramilitary forces and many NGOs helping us.

Our family was also growing happily. Sonya had moved to Gurgaon after her wedding and she was blessed with a baby boy, Ayaan, in September 2005.

No to Offers

Sometime in 2005, I got a surprise call from S.S. Sidhu, the then Governor of Manipur, offering me the post of Chairman of the Manipur Public Service Commission. I declined it after consulting with my family as we were happily settled in Delhi post-retirement and did not want to go there for another five years. A similar thing happened in 2010 when I got a call from Sanjay Panda, Chief Secretary of Tripura, at the behest of Tripura Chief Minister Manik Sarkar, offering me the post of Chairman of the Police Accountability Commission of the state—I had to turn this down too.

Member of the Monitoring Committee

In an interesting development, one day in May 2006, I received a message from Chief Justice Vijender Jain of the Delhi High Court, whom I had met briefly once at an airport, asking me to see him in his chamber. Intrigued, I went to meet him. To my surprise, he asked me to be a member of the Monitoring Committee of the High Court to take action against unauthorized constructions and public encroachments in Delhi which were going on unabated as the MCD was not taking any action. A Public Interest Litigation by an NGO was the trigger for this case in the High Court. His Bench, along with Justice Rekha Sharma, had appointed some advocates as Court Commissioners. R.S.

Gupta of the IPS, who was a batch junior to me and was earlier the Police Commissioner of Delhi, was the second member and our job was to coordinate the work of the Court Commissioners and other agencies to achieve the objective. I had known Gupta well as we both had served in the Delhi Police in the initial years of my service.

The Commissioner of the MCD was asked to provide us with an office, staff, transport, honorariums and other essentials. Our office was opened in a school in Lajpat Nagar. It was a challenging task, but we all went about it with missionary zeal. The Court Commissioners were advocates of repute and started doing their job in right earnest. They were Sidhartha Mridul (now a judge of the High Court), Kirti Uppal, Pushkar Sood, Sanjeev Bhandari, Sanjay Bansal, Rakesh Khanna, Sanjeev Ralli, Akshay Bipin and Arvind Gupta.

It was a demanding task because we were up against many interests—the violators, the corrupt, the pushers, the politicians with their own agenda, the officialdom—but together we made an impact. Land worth thousands of crores was extricated from the encroachers and chunks of unauthorized construction removed, including big slum clusters. We were all over the media. We ruffled many feathers but no one could do much against us as we had the protection of the court. Nobody would dare approach us with any recommendation. Ultimately, a fallout did occur. One day my house in Saket was vandalized by a group of unidentified people when I was away. My wife and daughter Sonya were at home and narrowly escaped getting injured. I refused to be cowed down and was strongly supported by the Chief Justice.

In the open hearings in the court, the officialdom had to cut a sorry figure many a time over our findings and action. We also gave many suggestions to the court which were helpful in the long run. The most surprising thing was that very few people were booked for violations and then action against those booked was totally missing. Once we sat down to assess the situation, we found out that it would take the authorities several decades to take action against those already booked.

In the court, the MCD brought the best known lawyers, such Harish Salve, Abhishek Singhvi, Arun Jaitley, Mukul Rohatgi, R.R. Prasad, to name a few, to put forward its arguments against us but even they couldn't cut much ice. I presented our case quite a few times in the High Court. It was a great learning experience personally and we discovered a lot about the functioning of the courts—both good and bad. The Court Commissioners deserve a compliment for doing an excellent job in various zones. The sincere senior officers of the MCD, DDA and other governmental organizations had a difficult time in the meetings with us because of their other compulsions, such as working with corrupt officials who had vested interests.

Since violence against us—a few Court Commissioners also had to face hostility—didn't work, the vested interests then thought of working on the judiciary to get rid of the Monitoring Committee they were so uncomfortable with. It took them time, but they finally succeeded after Chief Justice Jain went away to the Punjab and Haryana High Court as Chief Justice. Slowly but surely, they managed to get our committee wound up. We had worked from May 2006 to September 2008 with some success, but encroachments and unauthorized structures were back with vengeance after our departure.

During this period, Manika was blessed with baby boys—Aadit in 2006 and Avi in 2008. We were now proud grandparents of six grandchildren, four boys and two girls.

Gymkhana Club

Meanwhile, I started taking an interest in the activities of the Gymkhana Club. I had been its member since 1977. Starting from 2008, I contested elections to the general committee of the club for three years and won each time. I presided over the Administration Committee and Works Committee, respectively, apart from being a member of various other committees. It was an enriching experience and I contributed whatever I could. After a mandatory gap of two years, I contested for the position of the president of the club and lost badly as I refused to spend money on lavish parties for members/voters as a matter of principle. But in the Gymkhana Club elections, it was not possible to win unless vast amounts of money were spent, just like you can't win the municipal, assembly and parliamentary elections in the country if lavish funds are not used. But I have no regrets. The Gymkhana Club has been a great gift for socialization where I have picked up many lifetime friends.

Eminent Citizen

The Mahatma Gandhi National Rural Employment Guarantee Act (MGNREGA), 2005, giving guaranteed employment to the needy in rural areas, was in full swing. The Government of India led by Prime Minister Manmohan Singh of the Congress and the UPA had brought out this revolutionary Act, giving solace to millions. The government also appointed about 60 persons as 'Eminent Citizens' to look into its functioning in the country. I happened to be on the list and worked in this capacity for two years. During that period, I visited Gujarat quite a few times and found that the scheme worked well there. There was hardly any corruption and the needy were getting work on demand as laid down in the law. However, my reports stating these facts about Gujarat were not liked by the powers that be as a different political party was ruling at the Centre.

Training Aspiring Civil Servants

When the Monitoring Committee was being wound up, my friend and colleague R.S. Gupta took me to visit an organization called Samkalp, with which he was associated, its main aim being free coaching to aspirants for the written examination and interviews that were part of the civil services entrance examination. By then, I had been to the UPSC on a couple of occasions to be part of the panel for the final selection of candidates for the civil services.

Since I had that experience, I gladly joined Samkalp for this noble social cause, guiding the aspirants for interviews. It is honorary work that I still do and love. I am a part of its panels for such interviews every year and there are many retired, and even serving, civil servants and other professionals who are helping too. Every year, they coach a large number of candidates and definitely more than half of those who qualify for the interview make it to the final list, earning Samkalp a respected name. For the work I did for Samkalp, I was honoured with the 'Guru Samman' by M. Venkaiah Naidu, Vice-President of India in July 2018 at a function held by the organization in New Delhi.

Interestingly, some other institutes doing the same work commercially opened their doors for me. In addition, I started helping other institutes by conducting indoor classes on Internal Security and Disaster Management for written examinations, besides taking orientation classes for aspiring candidates, encouraging them and giving them tips on how to work and succeed in the examination. I have also visited different cities in India on behalf of some institutes and addressed hundreds of students. In this area I have made many friends—administrators, teachers and co-panellists from different services and professions—who have enriched my life.

International Committee of the Red Cross

In the meanwhile, I was appointed as a consultant to the Delhi-based office of the Nobel Prize-winning organization, the International Committee of the Red Cross (ICRC), on the recommendation of a senior colleague who had worked for them for many years and had decided to quit due to age. I have been working for them for almost six years and my basic job is to conduct training, again a field that I love, and teach subjects like human rights and crowd management with an international perspective, keeping ICRC guidelines and rules in mind. I have visited different places in India in this connection.

Association with the Education Sector

One of my younger neighbours from Bharat Nagar, Ashok Chitkara, who I fondly call Shoki, did us proud. Starting from humble beginnings, he went to Chandigarh to do his BEd, married a classmate, did his PhD in maths and became an expert teacher holding classes in the early morning for aspiring engineering and other students, including children of the bureaucracy and other well-known people. By sheer hard work, today he has under his belt two universities named Chitkara University (in Punjab and Himachal Pradesh). He is a well-known name in Chandigarh and his universities have tie-ups with some of the best universities in the world. He also publishes advertisements for his universities in the *Time* magazine. He says that I was his inspiration when he used to see me in the uniform of an IPS officer. Of course, I had taught him and Hardev, the person dealing with Japanese tourists whom I have mentioned earlier. I used to give lessons to younger students in evening classes held in a temple in Bharat Nagar as social service when I was studying for my graduation. Like Hardev, Shoki kept in touch and requested me to visit him at least once, so I did so.

When I went to Chandigarh for a meeting with the DGP Punjab, I called him on the phone to tell him that I would like to meet him. I had by then a vague idea that he was doing well but never in my wildest dreams did I think that he had been so successful. To my pleasant surprise, he promptly arrived in his Mercedes car, took me to his sprawling bungalow and showed me around his educational institutions. I am so proud of him. Later, on his insistence, I took my wife to Chandigarh to meet him and we were treated with tremendous regard and affection. He asked me to be a member of the Governing

Board of the first university that he had started and I gladly accepted his offer. Another youngster from Bharat Nagar who has made the colony and me proud is Vijay Kranti, a well-known journalist and expert on India-Tibet-China issues and the Dalai Lama.

I also know another Shoki (Ashok Vohra) who was a librarian in BPR&D when I was working there, and now runs a big business of petrol pumps in Mumbai. With hard work, drive and passion, he has achieved a lot. He is like a younger brother and I stay with him whenever I go to Mumbai.

Then I got associated with the well-known Salwan schools in Delhi. As they say, one thing leads to another. Sushil Salwan, Chairman of the famous Salwan Education Trust that has been running many schools in the Delhi-NCR region since Independence, is a leading advocate. I came into his contact while working in the Monitoring Committee when he came to meet me professionally on behalf of a client. During my Monitoring Committee days, he asked me to be the Chief Executive Officer (CEO) of his Trust. His grandfather had started a school in Peshawar, now in Pakistan, in the pre-Independence era and when the family moved to Delhi after the Partition, land was allotted for schools to be started in the Rajender Nagar area. His father was the Chairman of the Trust and the mantle had been passed on to him. Somehow I couldn't accept his offer then.

About five years later, he asked me to be the Chairman of two of their schools in an honorary capacity, a position with no pay or perks. I gladly accepted this offer and am still working in that capacity. This too was a learning experience as acquiring knowledge never ends. And in my own humble way, I am contributing whatever I can for the improvement of education. Occasionally, it is a pleasure for me to take classes on soft skills for students, teachers and even their relatives, all without fees. It always gives me happiness to share my experiences. I also firmly believe that learning and using soft skills—public speaking and communication skills just being two such skills—can improve one's life and career. I also wrote a book, *Tips for Personality Development*, which has been received well.

I accepted the Salwan school offer primarily because of my love for the education sector. Since childhood, I wanted to be a teacher. Later, I had the opportunity to open the CRPF Public School and I loved that venture, simultaneously learning a lot about schools. My foray into training corporates and civil service aspirants is part of my inclination towards education and I draw immense satisfaction from it.

Social Scientist

By default, I also became a social scientist! My friend and the well-known eye specialist, Dr Mahipal Sachdev of the Centre for Sight, asked me one day about the name of the NGO that I was running. He was referring to 'Vastradan'. He informed me that in accordance with legal requirements, he had to appoint an Ethics Committee for his hospital and it was mandatory for a social scientist to be a member. He said that since I was running an NGO, I was a social scientist according to their definition. He included me in the Ethics Committee and later, I became the co-Chairman. Interestingly, he was paying me an honorarium for attending these meetings as laid down by the rules. It was a great experience to be a member of the Ethics Committee. I worked for two years in it.

I have been associated with another hospital also, Jaipur Golden Hospital in Rohini, Delhi, owned by the trust of a transport company of the same name. My father-in-law, by virtue of his being shareholder of the company, was a trustee. After his demise sometime back, my brother-in-law Satish Khanna has filled up that position. Whenever needed, I have given a helping hand to them. Personally, for me and my family that hospital and its excellent professional specialists in various fields have been, and are, a great help in times of need.

Tourism Abroad

As already mentioned earlier, my wife and I are very fond of travelling. Having seen almost the whole of India during my service career, on and off duty, we decided to visit one or two countries each year after retirement. We started in 2006 and by now have visited many countries and always with well-known tourist agencies. It is a joy and opportunity to gain more knowledge when one sees different landscapes, peoples, cultures, foods, historical buildings and their heritage. However, our visits have suddenly come to a halt for the last three years, first, due to some health issues and then because of the Covid pandemic since 2020. Hopefully, we will be able to resume our trips soon once these viruses leave us.

Other Activities

I have been busy, of course at my own pace, with some other activities like reading books (mainly autobiographies of successful people in the world and self-help books)—a pastime I have been fond of since my childhood, occasionally writing a book (I have already written 13 books so far—the present one, hopefully, will be the last), writing articles for newspapers/magazines, listening to and delivering lectures, participating in TV debates, working with a few organizations, etc.

Besides, I spend a lot of time now on my body and mind and I am busy with my regular walks and yoga, besides practising Vipassana meditation. I have picked up a bit of golf and occasionally go to play.

There are a lot of social activities for me and my wife as our children and grandchildren are in Delhi–NCR too as are many relatives and friends. We were regular visitors to the Gymkhana Club also but due to the pandemic all these activities had been restricted to quite an extent. The activities have picked up again.

Overall, life is good. Of course, there are occasional health problems, but no serious complaints so far.

Chapter 13

Reflections

I have lived a life of more than three quarters of a century and it roughly coincides with the life of independent India since 1947—we both have come a long way. But I am not tired, or maybe, just a little. Overall, it has been a good journey with ups and downs, just as it is for everyone.

Personally, in a way, I have lived life across many centuries. When I look back, my life in my childhood seems to be centuries apart today with big shifts on the way. Starting from a refugee camp where six of us were sharing one small *kutcha* room, we became more comfortable when we were allotted a quarter in a refugee colony camp with two rooms, each opening into a small veranda, along with a bathroom and a toilet, with asbestos sheets as a roof. Eventually I moved to roomy flats and later bungalows with gardens, which has been a big change. Though I am back to a flat now, it is a modern one with all the amenities. From sweepers, including females, carrying our excrement on their heads (what a shame it was though I didn't realize it then) to modern toilets with efficient flush systems has been a metamorphosis. Seeing an English toilet seat when I was in the ninth standard and not understanding what it was to have such seats in bathrooms at home has been a huge change too.

A handpump to get water was a big luxury when I was a child and luckily for us in those times, we also had one towel and one soap for the whole family. I have moved over to taps with running water available round the clock, shampoos, shower gels, creams, and scores of towels for each member of the family. From bathing in the open in winter under a handpump to hot water from geysers in the cosiness of a modern bathroom attached to the bedroom is quite some progress.

In those days, I had no choice but to walk, and that was how I went to school—walking about 3 kilometres one way daily. From that to a bicycle to a bus to a scooter to a jeep to a second-hand Fiat car to a new Ambassador and then to the latest brands of luxury cars culminating in the fully automatic Baleno now has been a transformation. And from flying in a small Dakota to a helicopter to big modern streamlined aircrafts, and from economy class to business class and then to first class has been a huge jump. And from aircrafts waiting for me as an SP, to cars going up to the planes, to seeing off passengers from the inside the aircrafts, to now waiting in long queues to get a boarding pass, from being upgraded to business class generally without any additional cost, to now travelling only economy class is like going through a revolving door.

From studying under the dim light of kerosene lamps and street lights to getting electricity for the first time at home at the age of 18 years was thrilling. From a radio to a black and white TV to a colour TV, from limited programmes to round-the-clock programmes and now OTT platforms, from listening to cricket commentary at a *paan* shop on a radio to watching matches live in any part of the world has been nothing short of a miracle.

Where food is concerned, it has been a journey from a *mohalla dhaba* to the finest five-star hotels, from the lowly to the finest restaurants, from home-cooked *dal-roti* to the choicest cuisines. And from picking up food items from small shops to ordering food online and indulging in the luxury of home delivery has been revolutionary.

From very few clothes and homemade sweaters hung on the walls on nails to the finest suits in the most modern wardrobes has been a big change. From a shortage of money restricting us to buying only essentials (though we never felt poor or wanted to have more) to the ability to buy anything that we like—for example, from never buying shoes costing more than Rs 100 to buying expensive pairs worth, say, Rs 16,000 has been a big change. From no help at home to a battery of helpers and now again back to self-help has been full circle.

It is hard not to look back on the years passed and reflect on how different everything is now. Twenty years ago, the world was a completely different place than it is today—from a local family doctor to consulting top specialists in top hospitals and from homemade remedies to modern medicines; from no phone to getting one after a wait of three years to mobile phones in pockets; from writing letters and telegrams to emails to WhatsApp, Instagram and Twitter; from going to a photography studio to get a photograph clicked to taking your own photos and capturing special (or not so special) moments round the clock with mobile phones; from booking for railway journeys by going personally to the ticket counter and paying electricity bills after standing in long queues to doing these online from the comfort of one's home; from playing the role of a Police Inspector in a bus conductor's uniform to being a real police chief has been a metamorphosis as has been rising from being a mediocre student to the IPS to the selection panel for the civil services to being the Chairman of public schools and on the governing body of a university. Likewise, growing from a shy, introvert boy who couldn't stand on a stage to an extrovert good speaker and training others too, growing from a student of a government school to a boy who learnt the English language only in the fifth standard to speak and even write books and articles in English and participate in TV debates, using this language has been a big change.

Seeing marriages being performed in homes and simple settings with elaborate rituals attended by guests staying for days during weddings, including my own, shifting to banquet halls and luxury hotels with all rituals thrown out of the window are matched in deaths also, as the thirteenth day of mourning or *kriya* has given place to the *uthala* on the fourth day as people have no time and patience to follow these customs.

From holding the lowest position to the highest in the government has been a sea change for me. From meeting a locally-elected councillor to meeting chief ministers, governors, prime ministers and presidents, even attending dinners and parties at Raj Bhawans and Rashtrapati Bhawan, from witnessing the Independence Day proceedings among a crowd to being seated on the ramparts of the Red Fort in an official capacity, from being able to visit just a few areas in Delhi to seeing almost the whole of India and many countries of the world has been a big jump.

When I was in Mount Abu undergoing training in the National Police Academy, we were told that most of us would retire as a DIG as each state in India had only one IG as the police chief and only a few of us could attain that rank. From there to become a DGP and a state police chief has been another big jump. Thus, I turned out to be an unlikely police chief—first, because I got into this profession without dreaming about it and second, because I became a chief.

Other leaps and bounds from the primitive to technology have been: from struggling to learn typing at a young age to now using the keyboard on Microsoft Word with a good speed, and the use of computers, smartphones with different apps; paying with coins and paper notes to transferring money in seconds and making payments easily through apps like Paytm; buying things when one had savings, now there are instant loans; from rare telephones to STD booths to phones in the pocket now. Similarly, I have seen the emergence of stencils for making photocopies, then photocopiers, telex machines, fax machines; from typewriters to word processors to Microsoft Word; from tape recorders and transistors to recordings on mobile phones; from VCRs and cassettes and tapes to their vanishing; from floppy discs to CDs to pen-drives; from newspapers only to round-the-clock live news on channels and phones; from seeing the first clumsy computer in a huge room to desktops to laptops and now fingertips on mobile phones; from making trunk calls from one part of India to another taking three days and Rs 60 per minute for a call abroad to making instant video calls on WhatsApp today has been unbelievable.

I have seen tremendous changes in the film industry. From black and white films, to seeing two reels in colour for first time in the 1960 movie *Mughal-e-Azam;* from ordinary theatres to plush cinema halls, from pictures being shown in cinema halls to OTT platforms now; from discreet love being shown in films to open western-style kissing, from showing traditional conservative relationships to modern-day bonding; from indoor shooting of films to shooting with an evolving technology at exotic locations in India and abroad—the list of changes is endless.

I have only given an illustrative indication of the sea change from my childhood days to the present. I know I will see more as long as I live since technology is moving ahead fast. I have also changed over the years in many ways, sometimes as a natural process, sometimes after my efforts to improve myself, but am still connected to my roots, values, close relations and friends of my childhood whatever their financial or social status has been and is because ultimately they are my lifeline. I have succeeded, no doubt, in many ways with hard work but more than my effort, it has been the helping hand of God and my well-wishers—that is my firm belief.

Our country has made great strides though there are still darker areas. But today we are self-sufficient in foodgrains, milk, fruits, vegetables, among other items, which we even export after meeting the demands of a much increased population. Comparing it with the situation when we were hand to mouth and depending on PL 480 wheat from the USA in the early 1960s, living from ship to mouth, India has come a long way. Industrially, we have achieved a lot. In science, business, the arts, cinema and space technology, Indians have done wonders. We are the superpower of computer software and the pharmaceutical industry of the world. The contribution of our scientists in inventing vaccines and the efforts of the government to vaccinate over a billion people during the recent epidemic has been a huge achievement. The quantity of education imparted to our children has gone up by leaps and bounds, though the same cannot be said of quality. The same can be said about our engineering and medical colleges.

Poverty has reduced and healthcare is better than before. In the last 30 years, much has happened in India's infrastructure. Its four components—transport, energy, telecom/communications and cities —continue to improve. We have an effective presence in space and continue to grow with space rockets, even with the Mars Orbiting Mission launched by the Indian Space Research Organization (ISRO) called Mangalyaan and spacecraft like Gaganyaan. Top world companies like Microsoft, Google, Twitter, IBM, Adobe, etc. have Indian leaders at the helm of affairs; some are ministers in other countries and Kamala Harris, Vice-President of the US, is of Indian origin. WHO's Chief Scientist and IMF's Chief Economist are Indian women, as was the CEO of Pepsi. The list is too long to be mentioned.

In defence, we are much stronger due to more infrastructure, local and imported machinery, planes and ships and a strong resolve. Today, we can stand up to China. India's international standing has improved and is a voice which cannot be ignored.

All these have been achieved by Indians on their own and different political parties in power have played their own roles in the development of the country. It has been a big joy to witness this story and to be a part of it. Of course, we have a long way to go and that we will. I am optimistic about that.

There has been downslide also. Poverty and unemployment are still rampant. So are inequalities, illiteracy, communal tensions, atrocities on women, people belonging to the Scheduled Castes and Scheduled Tribes, children and senior citizens. Even this is a long list and shows the failures of the rulers. While democracy has done a lot of good to the country and kept the country unified, the system of fighting elections with money to get votes has damaged the society. For most politicians and political parties, it is self-interest, of the individual, family and party that comes first, centring on money. It is only if they have the inclination and money is left in the state coffers that they do something for the country. Selfishness and greed pervade the society, leading to evading and flouting laws and rules.

We have not been able to solve some problems for decades like terrorism in J&K, Maoist violence in many states and insurgency in some states of the North-East. Problems have been lingering on and serious statecraft has not been attempted to solve these problems from a long-term point of view.

The police has been cut to size. It continues to be under the control of the state politicians—policing being a state subject—and has become almost a private army of the politicians in power. It has been ruined in this way, with no respect for and justice given to the common man. It is affecting internal security adversely. Hence, there is an urgent need for police reforms, including the police force accountable to the rule of law and not politicians; having an exclusive Ministry of Internal Security at the Centre with more security professionals at policy and implementation levels; reducing the strength of the armed police at the Centre and states and increasing the strength and resources of the civil police as the growth of the armed police has outstripped the civilian force.

It has many administrative problems such as a lack of updated resources in many areas which need to be looked into, including on the technological front as cybercrimes have gone up considerably. The police leadership also has to stand up.

Similarly, the bureaucracy has been made subservient. No wonder, many among the police and bureaucracy join hands with the rulers who can damage their careers; it is not the other way round, even though it is legally possible. Of course, there are honourable exceptions at the IAS and IPS levels. Most of them are IIT graduates and doing a great job, but handling politicians is a tough call for them and most of them have no respect for these leaders. The concept of committed bureaucracy was started in early 1970s by the then Prime Minister Indira Gandhi. I was, perhaps, one of the early victims of this, a concept that has no place in a democracy and must stop.

The judicial system is under tremendous pressure. Crores of cases are pending in courts at all levels of the judiciary. The criminal justice system is badly broken. Comprehensive steps should be taken to ensure that the system works faster and more efficiently.

Respect for each other among politicians has also vanished—name calling has become the order of the day. Disgracing others is more important than the good of the county and nobody appreciates the good work done by a party or an individual. Social platforms have become like weapons for them, and, internationally, many people and ideologies support harmful elements in India. The credibility of state institutions like Parliament and Assemblies, the executive and judiciary also has taken a big hit.

But there is still hope. There are quite a few well-meaning and hard-working politicians and Indians of all hues, especially young men and women. Technology is becoming an effective aid in governance and is being used extensively, helping millions in various areas. It is continuously changing and new technological creations like 5G and artificial intelligence are coming up. We don't know what gadgets we will have in the future, but they will definitely change life for the better at an accelerated speed.

Managing India is no joke. In fact, it is many countries within one country with different cultures, religions, beliefs, languages, social structures, food and clothing. There is so much to do, including correction of many wrongs like written and taught history, all of which will take time. A span of 75 years in a country's life is minuscule. My observations will have many critics but mine is the perspective of just one person out of over a billion. Perhaps I deserve not be treated harshly on this account.

I feel particularly sad about the North-East, since I have served there for over a decade. A culturally rich place, it is populated with beautiful warm-hearted people. However, they have not got justice in the country. Enough attention has not been paid to the region's problems in a genuine manner and it continues to suffer. Nor has its history been given its due in the national curriculum. It gets almost no coverage at the Centre and is still considered alien. I can only appeal, pray and hope that justice is done to it with sensitivity and care.

Personally, my life has been good. I have committed mistakes, being human, and paid the price for which I did penance. Occasionally, they still bother me. Like other human beings, I have a few regrets. I have learnt lessons in life, spent a lot of time energy and money on self-improvement, but the process is not yet complete.

I am not a deeply religious person in the sense that I don't go to temples regularly or do formal prayers. Like my mother used to, my wife does, and for her sake I accompany her wherever she wants me to. In this matter, I am like my father. He used to say that the only religion we have in the world is to serve the human beings. I have followed this principle throughout my life. I also contribute to social causes whenever I am asked or when something comes my way and that gives great happiness and satisfaction. But I do believe in God.

I believe in three dictums learnt from others. First, when someone asks for help, he is actually seeing you as God's representative and God has given you the power to help him on His behalf, which is why you should. So be grateful when someone asks for help and do whatever you can. Second, the biggest help you can give anyone is to get him a job or ensure that he has the ways and means to earn a livelihood—this way you can look after a family for generations in all aspects. Providing, say, only a meal is good but giving a job or salaried work to someone is a million times better. Third, you are only a medium for whatever good or bad you do to others because what he gets is his luck, good or bad. People praise you when you do good deeds but criticize you when you do something wrong—but always remember you are just a medium. So don't be elated when praised, remain humble, and don't be dejected when criticized. The basic aim should be to do your best to help others and God will always reward you handsomely. It has happened in my case. In fact, He has given me much more than I ever deserved. And I have been a big beneficiary of generosity and help from scores of people, including my parents, teachers, relatives, friends and many unknown people. I am truly blessed and feel humbled. No quantum of saying thanks to them is enough.

I am also trying to reduce my expectations of others, trying not to expect them to thank me for what I have done for them or for reciprocity as in this world, generally, people don't do so. On my part I am trying to do this where others are concerned, but unfortunately, there is still a long way to go.

My special salute is to my country which has given me a lot.

Everything needed for existence—shelter, food, education and especially opportunities to do well—were given on a platter. I wouldn't have reached where I did in my personal and professional life, but for this grace. I have done the best I could with my limited capability and in humility to serve the people of the country in whatever small role I was assigned.

I must have hurt some people in the course of my life. I can only seek forgiveness but I couldn't have avoided it as it was a part of my thinking or job. There was never any malice in my heart.

Overall, in the autumn of life, I am happy, healthy and feel young at heart. My health depends on God and on me, a joint venture. I do my part in taking care of my health by regular yoga, walk and Vipassana meditation. Besides, I play golf sometimes. I have to make an effort for myself, although genes may play a part in how one's health is, and I leave the rest to destiny. I have a safe, comfortable home in which I am living happily with my wife on a pension that is enough for us, and my children are well settled.

In this world, I am a very small actor and have tried to play the minor role assigned to me to the best of my ability. Of course, it was a performance with ups and downs. I hope to end my innings gloriously, but leave that to God, who I believe will decide at His own timing. My only prayer is that I wouldn't like to be physically or mentally challenged and I don't want to be bedridden or a burden to my family so long as I live. I don't want to be dependent on anybody in my old age. I pray that God will oblige. As long as I can, I will continue working for the welfare of others and praying for the well-being of everybody, including my motherland.

Jai Hind

Index